DIAMONDS
IN THE
ROUGH

TONY LUCADELLO in a familiar stance scouting young players for the Philadelphia Phillies.

THE LEGEND AND LEGACY OF
TONY LUCADELLO

DIAMONDS
IN THE
ROUGH

DAVID V. HANNEMAN

DIAMOND BOOKS ★ **Austin, Texas**

FIRST EDITION

Copyright © 1989
By David V. Hanneman

Published in the United States of America
By Diamond Books
An Imprint of Eakin Publications, Inc.
P.O. Drawer 90159   ★   Austin, TX 78709-0159

ISBN 0-89015-666-2

Library of Congress Cataloging-in-Publication Data

Hanneman, David V.
    Diamonds in the rough.

    1. Lucadello, Tony, 1913–1989. 2. Baseball — United States — Scouts — Biography.
  I. Title.
GV865.L79H36   1989   796.357′092′4   [B]   88-33594
ISBN 0-89015-666-2

In fond memory of Tony Lucadello,
baseball's greatest scout.
His legacy will live on in the hearts
of every man who has ever played the game.

Tony Lucadello with Mike Schmidt at festivities honoring Mike's 500th homerun, Veterans Stadium, Philadelphia.

Contents

vi

Preface

I took a trip once, a long and memorable trip up to northern Ontario to look at a pitcher in the little mining camp of Timmons. I drove my car from Fostoria to Detroit, caught a plane to Toronto, then took a train to the northern reaches of the province. The mining camp was so far back in the sticks that I had to hire a guide and a canoe to cover the last few miles.

It was late in the day when I finally arrived, so I decided to stay overnight and work the boy out in the morning. In the meantime I was given a tour of the camp. I was given special coveralls and taken to a large building where a conveyor belt brought up the ore-rich gravel and dirt from the mines. There it was cleaned, separated, and smelted. Silver was poured into ingots in one separate room; gold in another.

I had to be washed down when I left the building because a light film of gold dust had covered my clothes while I'd been inside.

I never did sign that pitcher from Timmons, Ontario, but I never forgot that trip. I was willing to go anywhere to find major league talent. In my travels I've met many warm and wonderful people. I may not have mentioned all of them in this book, but I do want to thank them all for their friendship, their support, their helpfulness, and their love. It's left on me a film of gold dust I hope never washes off.

This book is not about me. It is for me. It is my way, hopefully, of recognizing some very special people.

I have signed forty-nine major league ballplayers in just over forty years of scouting. People say I'm successful. I pray, though, that I never become so vain as to think that I am the beginning and the end of that success. I am just one link in the chain that unites all of baseball.

I love the people of baseball as much as I love the sport. It is to those people, at every stage of the game, that I dedicate this book.

I feel I owe the most to Jack Sheehan, who served as the compass of my career as a baseball scout. He gave me a start and offered needed direction when I got into the business. Everything I achieved is because of him.

I have been fortunate to work under excellent management: P. K. Wrigley and Jim Gallagher with the Chicago Cubs, and Robert and Ruly Carpenter, Paul Owens, Gene Martin, and Dallas Green with Philadelphia. My own part-time scouts — my eyes and ears around the Midwest — were instrumental in my success. Without men like Casey Lopata (southern Michigan), Pete Mihalic (northwestern Ohio), Bob Kowaleski (northern Michigan), Ed French, Rich Sander (Cincinnati), Norm Kramer (northern Indiana), Don Shaw (Columbus), Donnie Beckhart (Kentucky, southern Indiana), Carl Lowenstine, Ken Elam (Illinois), Larry Grefer (Cincinnati), Harry Weinbrecht, and Dick Hopkins I could never have been as thorough in my scouting.

In my career as a scout I developed a great relationship with several outstanding college coaches, including Bob Wren (Ohio University), Bob Miller (University of Detroit), Dick Finn (Ohio State, Toledo), Ron O'Strike and Roger Corell (Eastern Michigan), Stan Sanders (Toledo), and Don Purvis (Bowling Green State University).

My incentive for wanting this book written, though, was to bring attention to the people in the background, the unknown giants who never share the spotlight. They are the parents, coaches, and sponsors who take money out of their own pockets and devote their own precious time to amateur baseball for one reason: because they love the sport. It makes no difference to them if it's high school, American Legion, Connie Mack, Acme, Babe Ruth, or sandlot, they give of themselves so that young men across the country have the opportunity to play baseball. Few receive much recognition, but I'd like to mention several whom I truly respect: Dayton's Ted Mills, who has won over 700 games and several national titles with his Parkmoor Restaurants and Cassis Packaging Company teams; Joe Hawk of Cincinnati's Bentley American Legion Post; Joe Hayden and his Midland Redskins; Hal Pennington, who won over 1,000 amateur games as a manager; Mike Adray, one of the biggest sponsors of amateur athletics in Detroit; Kokomo's Bob Ronk; Fr. Cullen of Assumption High School in Canada; along with Glenn Sample (Cincinnati), Dick Templin (Indianapolis), Pop Frankel (South Bend), Tom Noland (Dearborn), Joe Cooper (Marshall, Michigan), Linc Hackim (Akron), Herm Kander (Toledo), Jim Hardman (Piqua), Lou Brunswick (Coldwater), and Jim Kin and Don Edwards.

Some will be mentioned in this book. Some will not. And there are many others I have neither the memory nor space to devote equal recognition. I sincerely hope that the role these people play in amateur baseball is appreciated. I am a firm believer that great athletes are not born to greatness. I feel it is something they achieve through hard work, desire, dedication, and the support and training they received early in their careers.

This book is not a chronological autobiography but a collection of excerpts from my career as a baseball scout. As I relate my own experiences, whether it be a personal exploit or the signing of a big-name player, I hope to offer a glimpse into the entire realm of scouting.

I also hope Elizabeth Riordan likes it. A secretary in our organization, Elizabeth has been after me for years to get all my stories and experiences down in print. I guess I owe this book to her.

— TONY LUCADELLO

Acknowledgment

A special thanks to Thom Mudrick, associate scout for the Philadelphia Phillies and my friend, without whose hard work and perseverance this book would never have been published.

— Tony Lucadello

Introduction

In the tiny den of a quaint white house on the outskirts of Fostoria, Ohio, Tony Lucadello reigned over the biggest little kingdom in the world.

His domain was Lilliputian. A furnace covered one whole corner of the kingdom. A single bed, a desk, and a bureau dominated the rest. Thank God that, in stature, the ruler fit the premises. His little-old-winemaker frame glided easily under ductwork the average man had to stoop to conquer.

The domain was universal. The outside world peered in through the picture portrait windows of Lucadello's past. There, in the center of one wall, was Mike Schmidt. And next to him Grant Jackson. Farther to the right was Fergie Jenkins and Tom Underwood, and below them Larry Hisle and Toby Harrah. About them were clustered the likes of Mike Marshall, Dave Roberts, Jim Essian, Todd Cruz, Bill Nahorodny, Larry Cox, and a host of others.

If the names sound familiar, they should. All are major league baseball players and all were signed to their first professional contract by Lucadello. In over forty years of beating the bush for that fly-speck of talent, Lucadello discovered and signed forty-nine major league players. His total should top fifty when some current minor leaguers get called up.

In baseball circles, Lucadello is well known. He has been referred to as the "scout's scout" and the "Babe Ruth of scouting." A measure of his status in the baseball community came a few years back when Birdie Tebbetts, a former manager of Cleveland, Cincinnati, and Milwaukee Braves and a member of the Baseball Hall of Fame Veterans Committee, recommended that scouts also be considered for induction into baseball's grand hall. Among those he mentioned for the possible honor was Lucadello.

Scouting was an occupation of fate for Lucadello, a man born in Thurber, Texas, in 1913, raised in street-tough Chicago, and weaned on the sandlot baseball of the Midwest. The dirt diamond fields of Roseland were his classroom, and the sheer love of competition his teacher. For three years Lucadello was shortstop for the All Nations team in Roseland. He then spent two seasons with Verhoveys and another with International Harvester.

In 1936, when Branch Rickey decided to expand the St. Louis Cardinals' minor league system, a franchise was opened in Fostoria, Ohio. Lucadello, figuring it was time to try his hand at minor league baseball, went over for a tryout and made the team. For six years Lucadello played in the Ohio State League, mostly with the Fostoria Redbirds. The team occasionally played exhibition games in Chicago, and though Lucadello never was offered a major league contract he at least impressed one Windy City team in another respect.

The Chicago Cubs was one of the last major league organizations to develop an extensive minor league system. Until 1943 their major source of talent was a Class AAA team club in Los Angeles called the Angels. But it was just one team, and there was just so much room on the roster. When the Cubs decided to expand their organization in 1943, they named Jack Sheehan as their farm director. Sheehan's first move was to find some part-time scouts who could comb the Midwest, and one of the first men he approached was Lucadello. Sheehan had seen Lucadello when he was player-manager with the Redbirds and Tiffin Mud Hens and had been impressed with the man's spunky cockiness and baseball savvy.

That was the start. Lucadello's determination and eye for real talent did the rest. In the beginning, Lucadello ran tryout camps. He'd bring forty or fifty prospects in each week and work them out. Upper Sandusky was his base of operations at the time, and when he found a ballplayer he liked he asked him to stay. That meant finding the kid a job, but that wasn't too hard to do. The war was still going on and there were many families that could use an extra hand. Several people put the young players up in their homes, where they could rent a room for a dollar a week and still have a little money left to live on.

Lucadello then begged, borrowed, and stole every piece of equipment he could get his hands on. Stuff others had thrown away he fixed, and uniforms others had worn out he patched. Gradually, he outfitted one team, then two. On weekends Lucadello still ran his tryout camps. On weekdays he worked out his teams, four hours a day. And whenever they could they played, against any and all competition. Soon they were beating all the teams in the area and branching out. Once, in Lima, they played the famed Kansas City Monarchs, the black team led by Satchel Paige, and lost by a run.

Although the Cubs left Lucadello on his own to develop his talent, some interesting reports were soon filtering up to the front office. Jack Sheehan called Lucadello to ask what was going on and Lucadello told him he was just doing the job he had been hired to do — find and train ballplayers. But the Cubs couldn't understand how Lucadello had done so well so fast. They wanted proof, so they asked him to select his best eighteen players and take them to Chicago for a matchup against the best players from the other minor league teams. Lucadello assembled his team, went to Chicago and, in a Saturday-Sunday doubleheader, swept all four games.

Impressed with the team and the man who had put it together, the Cubs offered several of the players contracts and Lucadello a position as a full-time scout. His scouting career began in earnest then. With the war coming to a close, and thousands of young men coming home, the sandlots and amateur programs were soon flooded with good, young talent. The need for scouts and more and better farm systems was becoming crucial. In the heart of that boom Lucadello thrived, signing twenty-three major leaguers for the Cubs in fourteen years.

What Lucadello didn't realize at the time was that while he was out scouting, others were out scouting him. Robert Carpenter had bought the Philadelphia Phillies in 1937, but after several lean years he was making some changes. Gene Martin was named farm director and Ross Miller was assigned his assistant. It was their job to monitor the young talent coming up from the ranks. From the University of Delaware, Robert Carpenter selected Mike Lutz to find the best scouts available. Lucadello, his success already well known, headed the list.

With the Cubs going through a transition period, Lucadello got his release from the club in 1957 and joined the Phillies. Twenty-six additional major leaguers later, he was still going strong when his life ended, just before the printing of this book, in 1989. Now these stories of Lucadello's career, told in his own words, will serve to carry on the legend of a truly great scout.

You can measure Lucadello's success as a baseball scout in the number of major leaguers he signed, or in the years he was in the business. But the real measure of his esteem comes from the men whose lives he touched.

"There's not a more sincere, hard-working scout than Tony Lucadello," said Larry Hisle, one of the greats Lucadello signed. "When I was in the minors with Jack Foreman we'd both get a letter from Tony every day. We were both a bit homesick and unsure of our careers, but every day there would be a note from Tony telling us to keep trying and not lose hope.

"Tony did that for all the players he signed, not just the high draft choices. It didn't matter to him if you were black or white or green. You were a human being, and he treated you with respect. He made you feel like family."

Baseball's
Greatest Catch

◆────────────────◆

You talk about some of the great baseball catches of all time and some classics come to mind:

· Brooklyn's Al Gionfriddo robbing Joe DiMaggio of a three-run home run in the sixth game of the 1947 World Series, a catch that preserved the Dodgers' 8–5 lead and forced a seventh game with the Yankees.

· Willie Mays racing to the deepest part of the Polo Grounds to make an unbelievable over-the-shoulder grab of Vic Wertz blast in the 1954 World Series opened between the Giants and Indians.

· A year later, in the final game of the 1955 World Series, Brooklyn's Sandy Amoros making an equally incredible catch, a desperation lunge and grab on Yogi Berra's fly ball down the left field line that saved the Dodgers 2–0 championship victory.

· The scintillating catches of Tommie Agee and Ron Swoboda in the 1969 World Series as the Miracle Mets capped their storybook season.

The highlight films document hundreds of brilliant catches, but labeling one "the greatest" is a toss-up. Why, even Tony Lucadello had a candidate for the honor.

Evenings are cool in Puerto Rico, once the hot Latin sun goes down. I had just finished my dinner in the large hotel where we were staying while running a huge tryout camp and clinic. I had developed a system where we could have between 500 and 800 players working out at one time and some of the Phillies' top personnel — Ruly Carpenter, Dallas Green, Paul Owens — had come down to watch. Tony Taylor and Tony Perez were helping me run the thing.

I was ready to call it a day when a waiter came by and said that Mr. Carpenter and his party wanted to see me on the patio. They had been swapping baseball stories, and knowing that I told a pretty good tale or two, they asked me to add one of my own.

"Come on, Tony," they said. "Tell us one of those great stories you have so many of."

"Well," I told them, "I'll tell you about the greatest catch ever made in baseball. You all probably think Willie Mays made the greatest catch in the 1954 World Series. But I saw one that was even better. And I ought to know. I'm the guy that made it."

They guffawed and laughed and such, but I was serious. So I said I'd tell the story, and then they could judge if it was the best catch ever made or not.

"It was back in 1936," I told them. "George Silvey was managing the Fostoria Redbirds, a Class D team affiliated with St. Louis, and me and my brother Johnny played on the team. It was our first year of pro ball, but we fielded a decent team: I was at short, Pete Wahonick at second, Ed Zipay, Zang Satulla, and Dave Danaher in the outfield, and George at first.

"We made a pretty good bid for the Ohio State League championship too. Tiffin, an affiliate of Detroit, just beat us out the first half of the season and won the second half when we got killed by injuries. Tiffin's big gun was a guy named Zeke Clements, a huge fella who belted forty-seven homers that season. Zeke plays a key role in this story.

"We got off to a quick start the second half of the season and opened a three-and-a-half-game lead. But like I said, injuries killed us. I sprained my ankle, Wahonick's arm swelled up and he couldn't play, and Zipay, who was hitting .412 with twenty-two homers at the time, broke his leg sliding into second and missed the last part of the season. A ten-game losing streak dropped us way out of first and we never got back in. We played Tiffin in the last game of the season, a game everyone thought would be for the title, but by then the Mud Hens had it wrapped up.

"Since that game meant nothing to the final standings, George decided to experiment a little bit. He moved a young newcomer into my spot at short, but since I was swinging a good bat at the time he kept me in the lineup and put me in center. I hadn't played the position before, so in between innings I'd do a little experimenting of my own. I'd come charging in like I was going to make a shoestring catch, or I'd race back like I was going for a deep fly.

"I also noticed that the outfield fence was a bit peculiar. Two-by-fours had been nailed across the fence posts and regular slat boards had been nailed on the outside of the two-by-fours. It must have been for advertising or something.

"I got the idea, as I was practicing running down long flies, that I could step on the lower two-by-four and reach way over the fence. I didn't think I'd ever have to during the game, but it was a handy piece of knowledge I sorta shoved in the back of my mind.

"That game didn't mean much in the standings, but there was a lot of pride at stake. We wanted to get revenge for being nosed out by Tiffin in both halves of the season and the Mud Hens wanted to prove they deserved the league crown.

"We scored a couple of runs early, but Tiffin rallied for a 3–2 lead. We scratched for the tying run, then went ahead 4–3 late in the game.

"Tiffin, though, got the leadoff man on in the bottom of the ninth, then sandwiched a hit and a walk around two outs. And with the winning run on second, Big Zeke Clements stepped to the plate.

"One ball our pitcher threw him, then another. The third pitch was a called strike, but Zeke, waiting for something fat, teed off on the fourth. Like a golf ball it took off, first on a line, then climbing into the twilight.

"Zeke's forty-eighth home run, everyone thought, would win the game. But I wasn't giving up. I raced back to the wall and looked up. Still too high. I stepped onto that two-by-four and reached up once more. But I saw the ball would clear my glove with room to spare.

"I was giving the game up for lost when, out of the corner of my eye, I saw a blur. A pigeon came streaking out of the dusk and flew smack into the path of the ball. Almost right over my head they collided, and at the last instant I stretched over the fence and made my catch.

"I jumped off that fence and thrust my glove in the air as the umpire signaled Big Zeke out. Then I took off running across right field.

"Nobody could believe I'd made the catch. Our guys were jumping all over each other and their team was just standing around, their heads hanging.

"Ol' George Silvey, though, wasn't going to let me get away. Good ol' frugal George, who ran the club on a shoestring and often made us fetch home run balls to be reused, wasn't going to let me sneak off with a good baseball, a souvenir of the game. After all, baseballs cost money, and that was a scarce commodity at our level.

"Like a linebacker George charged after me. And in the right-field corner, where I ran out of room, he made the tackle.

" 'Hand over the ball, Lucadello,' he yelled at me.

" 'I can't,' I told him. 'The ball went over the fence. I caught the pigeon.'

"Then I took the bird out of my back pocket, where I had stashed it, and showed him.

"I thought George might blow the whole thing right then and there but he didn't. He just gaped at the pigeon, reaching out as if to touch it, then pulling his hand back.

" 'Let's get out of here,' he finally mumbled, and we sauntered off the field with no one the wiser.

"We were a rowdy locker room that night, but after everyone had showered and dressed George quieted us down. He didn't say anything, just kept looking out the door to see if anyone was around.

"Finally, when everyone else had left the ballpark, George went to a toolshed around the corner and came back with a shovel. He marched us back on the field and began to dig up the batter's box. Right there, under home plate, we buried that pigeon good and deep.

"Most of the players just stood there and gawked. We didn't tell anyone right then that I had caught the bird instead of the ball. But then again, no one really asked either.

"One of the funniest things, though, is that after we buried the pigeon, George made us climb the fence and hunt up Big Zeke's home run. He just couldn't stand to lose a good baseball."

When I finished the story, Mr. Carpenter and the others were laughing so hard they were lying all over the patio. It was fifteen or twenty minutes before any of them could complete a full sentence without breaking up all over again.

They all agreed it was one of the best stories they'd heard, but they weren't sure I hadn't made it all up. Paul Owens said he had George Silvey's phone number and would call him to check it out.

"It's true. All of it," Silvey said. "But I sure wish Lucadello would quit telling the story. Every time he does, someone calls me in the middle of the night to see if it's true or not."

"Picking"
Apart the Pitcher

◆────────────────◆

There's a new aspect of athletics to be found in locker rooms from high schools to the major leagues. It's called sports psychology and deals with an athlete's mental feelings about himself and his sport.

Though most of the research into sports psychology has been recent, the idea isn't a new one. Tony Lucadello was practicing the art long, long ago, though not in the same sense. Tony used sports psychology on the opposition, not on himself, and in one instance he may have pulled off the biggest "psyche job" in baseball history. Again it was in 1936, and ironically it came against the same Tiffin Mud Hens team Tony had made his greatest catch against.

Back in '36 I was playing semipro ball with the Fostoria Redbirds, a Class D farm club of St. Louis that played in the Ohio State League. George Silvey was our manager and we had a pretty decent team except for our pitching.

We won our share of games — even made a run at the division title. But the Tiffin Mud Hens, an affiliation of the Detroit organization, was the class of the league. They had everything — pitching, hitting, and defense. Zeke Clements, their big first baseman, led the league in homers that year and they had a pitcher, Chuck Cronin, who won something like eighteen games, obviously the best pitcher in the circuit.

Cronin owned us that year. We never could beat him. All he had to do was throw his glove on the mound and we were done. But Chuck was a cocky ballplayer, make no mistake about it, and you could always get into an argument with him if you lipped off a little bit.

But I was kinda cocky too. I played shortstop for the Redbirds and I wasn't exactly the most mild-mannered guy on the squad. I thought I could afford to be cocky that year. I was hitting well over .350, and I thought nothing of spouting off about it now and then.

I had always hit Cronin well, but as a team we never had much luck against him. I thought a lot of our guys were intimidated by him. Somehow I had to figure a way to build up the confidence of my team, to pump 'em up so they could beat this Cronin guy. I wracked my brain for days, but it wasn't until a late-season match-up with the Mud Hens that an idea began percolating in my head. Shortly before game time, I put my plan into action.

In a lot of ballparks back then, and I guess in most of them today, the pitchers would warm up along the sidelines, the home team down the third base line, the visitors on the other side. Deep in the corners they put the outhouses, at least that's where they were back then. Before every game I'd stroll to the outhouse, always making sure to use the one on the other team's side of the field. And I'd always chat with the catcher as I passed by, just to say hi and howdy but really to get a look at the opposing pitcher, check his warmups, and get a line on him.

I knew Cronin was pitching that night, so as I strutted across the field I jammed a toothpick in my mouth. Then, after watching Cronin throw a few pitches, I sidled on over to the catcher.

"Doesn't look like he has it tonight, Joe," I said, just like I was making idle conversation.

The catcher just chuckled. Not loud, mind you, but loud enough to ruffle Cronin's fine feathers.

"Hey, you little sawed-off sonuvabitch," he yells. "What're you saying about me?"

"Easy, Chuck," I soothed. "I was just telling Joe here how you look a little slow tonight. From what I've seen you haven't got much on the ball. If you don't watch it you're gonna get hit bad tonight."

"Fat chance, Lucadello," he spat back. "I've been eating you guys up all season."

"Not me," I said, egging him on. "Here I am the leadoff man for these Redbirds, one of the littlest guys on the team, and there's no way you throw a strike past me. I've seen you at your best and still hit you. Face it, Chuck, you just ain't got it tonight. Hell, I could hit you with my eyes closed."

"Try it, runt, and I'll knock the bat right outta your hands."

"Now, Chuck, I can hit you and you know it. I can hit you any time I want. I could give you two strikes and I'd still get a hit."

Boy, 'ol Chuck was steaming after that. He ranted and raved and carried on so much I thought he was going to burst. He came charging at me, grabbed me by the shirt, and hauled back like he was going to take a punch.

"Go ahead and hit me, Chuck," I said calmly. " 'Cause that's the only way you're going to beat me . . . with your fists. You know you can't beat me throwing a baseball, not unless you throw at my head. Even then you're so slow I could just step out of the way.

"Tell you what, Chuck, to prove my point I'll put you through the test tonight. I'm gonna show you just how good you really are, and I'll show everybody just how good I am."

"Oh yeah? How?"

"Well, you see this here toothpick, Chuck?"

"Yeah, what about it?"

"It's like this, Chuck. I like to carry this toothpick around because it reminds me of you. I like to chew on it and every time I get a little spit on it I think of you and how easy it is for me to hit you. And when that toothpick gets good and wet it's hard to break. It may bend, but it won't split in two.

"That's what I do with my bats, too, Chuck. I spit on 'em and every time I do I think of how easy it is to hit your pitching. I don't rub my bats with bone like some of the guys. All I got to do is spit. That's why tonight I'm gonna hit you with this toothpick, Chuck. I'm gonna walk up to home plate with this little toothpick and I'm gonna show you I can hit your best pitch with it."

"Try it and I'll put it right between your eyes."

"You've tried, Chuck," I said. "But anybody can get out the way of your pitches. Sooner or later you're gonna have to come in with a good one and I'll get a piece of it. I may not knock it out of the park, but I'll get on base. I guarantee you of that."

"You gotta be nuts," he hollered. "You haven't got the guts to pull a stunt like that."

"You just watch me, Chuck. Joe here's heard the whole thing and he can verify it. He's gonna be right there to see there's no funny business. Besides, I don't need a gimmick to hit you, Chuck."

Then I spat on the toothpick, just for effect, and turned and headed for our dugout.

The game started a short time later and I led off. True to my word, I sauntered up there with nothing but that toothpick in my teeth.

"Where's your bat?" the ump asked.

"Right here," I said, showing him the toothpick. "That's my bat."

"Get serious, Lucadello," he said. "Get a bat and get back in the box or I'll start calling 'em."

"Go ahead," I said, grabbing that toothpick tightly in my left hand. "That big shot on the mound thinks he's the greatest pitcher in the world, but I'm gonna teach him a lesson."

The discussion had gotten pretty loud, drifting into our dugout and filtering up into the stands until there was a steady buzz of unanswered questions.

"Come on, Chuck," I yelled at the mound. "Whatsa matter? Can't you see this little toothpick in my hand? I said I was gonna hit you with it and here I am. Come on, hot shot, gimme your best pitch."

During his warmups, Chuck would come halfway to the plate for the return throw and mutter nasty little things under his breath. Now, with the umpire's call of "Play ball" still echoing through the stands, Chuck got a determined look on his face, went into his windup, and uncorked a screamer toward the plate. I expected him to come with his best pitch so I was ready. When I saw that hummer coming I grabbed that toothpick as hard as I could, nice and steady so he couldn't knock it out of my hands, and aimed for the pitch. It came over the plate like a bullet, but my aim was true. The ball nicked the toothpick and bent it over.

For a split second there was dead silence. Then I turned to the umpire and asked, "What's the call?"

He never hesitated. His right hand shot out and he bellowed, "Foul ball. Strike one."

"You see that, Chuck?" I yelled, holding that toothpick high in my hand. "All I had was a measly toothpick and I fouled off your best pitch. Imagine what I would have done with a real bat."

My teammates went nuts and the fans, caught up in the little drama, cut loose. Chuck charged off the mound at me, but thought better of it and backed off when my team started pouring out of the dugout.

My point made, I got a bat from the dugout and, on Chuck's first pitch after the bedlam died down, I hit a clean single to right. As I rounded first Big Zeke Clements picked me up, patted me on the back, and darn near kissed me. He wasn't the biggest fan of Chuck's either, being as cocky as he was, and couldn't believe someone had finally shown him up.

You might not believe it, but we knocked that guy out of the box in the first five innings. Chuck didn't beat us the rest of the year and we never, at least that season anyway, had trouble with him again. He was so psyched he didn't know how to pitch to us.

Chuck Cronin was, though, the best pitcher in our league. He later went into the army, put a fine team together and, ironically, came back to play us. Naturally, we got to talking about the toothpick incident and he said I could never do it again.

"You want me to try?" I asked.

Chuck thought about it a bit, then just shook his head no. I got three hits off of him that night, with a real bat in my hands and a toothpick — just in case — in my mouth.

Johnny Lucadello

♦——————————————————————♦

Each journey begins with a single step. For Lucadello, the journey into major league scouting began close to home, almost under his own roof as a matter of fact. The first major leaguer Lucadello signed was his own brother, Johnny.

I had played professional baseball with the Fostoria Redbirds since 1936, and one summer my brother Johnny came down to see me. My mother and sister had said he was getting into trouble in Chicago, shooting dice and things and hanging around with some bad characters. So I said he could spend the summer with me. I figured the change would do him good.

Johnny was only fifteen at the time, but George Silvey, our manager, said it was all right for him to work out with the Redbirds. It gave him something to do and kept him out of trouble, away from pool halls and such.

Johnny was young, but he was one helluva ballplayer. Always had been. Silvey was so impressed he recommended Johnny to the St. Louis Cardinals' front office. Because of his age, I said I'd handle the signing. I also had my eye on the $200 bonus that went with it. That was an awful lot of money in those days.

But Branch Rickey, general manager for St. Louis back then,

wasn't sold on Johnny. He suggested we send him to Rochester, New York, to work out for a week or so, sort of on a trial basis. So we packed Johnny up, put him on a train, and off he went to New York.

Johnny did well there too. But when he got back, Rickey still wouldn't spring for the $200 for me to put Johnny under contract. Since the deal didn't materialize, I didn't let Johnny sign with anybody. No one knew he wasn't under contract, even though he kept working out with the team. That type of thing was pretty customary in those days.

There came a series, though, when I hurt my ankle and Johnny filled in for me. Since I was a shortstop and Johnny a second baseman, they moved our regular second baseman to short and Johnny played his position. Played it well, too, and hit something like .268 or .270. Even when I got back in the lineup two weeks later, they still tried to slip Johnny in for me sometimes.

Well, the season ended, and Johnny and I headed home to Chicago. There we got ready for the annual all-star game between the best professional farm system players who lived in Chicago and inmates of the state prison at Joliet, Illinois state prison. It was like a benefit game and they always brought in a celebrity manager. That year it was Rogers Hornsby, the St. Louis Browns' manager, since he lived near Chicago.

On the day of the game, we all met Mr. Hornsby in front of the gates of the prison. We knew him. Heck, everybody knew Rogers Hornsby. But he didn't know us from the Seven Dwarfs. Because I was always talkative and such, though, he singled me out.

"Hey, you," he says. "You probably know more about these players than I do. How 'bout you making out the lineup for the game?"

We had Johnny on the roster, even though he wasn't under contract. And with me making out the lineup, naturally he got to start at second.

We got beat 2–1 that day. Only had four hits. But Johnny had three of them and Hornsby was impressed.

"Who's that kid signed with?" he asked me later.

"Nobody," I said.

"Why not?"

"'Cause Branch Rickey won't give me the $200 to sign him, that's why."

"You just leave it to me," Hornsby said. "I'll get you that $200."

So Rogers Hornsby got a hold of John Gilliland, the Browns' farm director, and a few days later he explains the deal to me.

"Listen," I tell him. "You just send that contract to me. And make sure you put the $200 with it. I'll take care of the rest."

My parents in Chicago knew nothing about baseball, nothing about these deals. All they wanted the boy to do was get a job and make some money. So when the contract came, I put my dad's name to it to okay it and that was it. I had signed my first ballplayer.

I signed a lot more players after that. Back then it wasn't unusual to sign ten ballplayers a season. But how many made it to the big leagues, I'm not real sure. The whole system was different then.

I do remember the first college player I signed who made it to the majors, a man named Wayne Terwilliger. He later coached with the Washington Senators when they had Ted Williams. And one of the things I'm proudest of is signing twenty-five major leaguers in twenty-five years with the Phillies.

But that first one, signing Johnny, was pretty special.

Johnny did real well too. He hit .338 in Class D ball in 1937 and .334 the next season in Class C. He hit better than .300 in Class B and the Texas League, and every year, near the end of the season, they'd bring him up to the big club for a week or two.

It was one of those times he was called up that Johnny hit two home runs in one game, one from the right side of the plate, one from the left. He was the first switch-hitter ever to do it.

Mickey Mantle once hit switch-hit homers in one game and the New York newspapers made a big deal about him being the first. But the St. Louis papers sent them the story of how Johnny had done it and they had to back off.

Maybe they were trying to get even. You see, when Johnny hit his switch-hit homers, he did it against the Yankees.

Cloak-and-Dagger Scouting:
The Signing of Mike Schmidt

◆———————————————◆

Since the mid-1970s, Mike Schmidt has been, without a doubt, one of the premier superstars of baseball.

Six times Schmidt has led the National League in home runs. When he won the home run crown in 1976, his third straight title, it marked the first time in twenty-four years a National League player had won the honor more than twice in succession.

A cornerstone of Philadelphia's rise to prominence in the mid- and late '70s, Schmidt powered the Phillies to a World Series championship in 1980 and was a unanimous selection as the National League's Most Valuable Player. It was only the second time in the history of the senior circuit that a player had been named on every ballot.

Following the strike-shortened 1981 season, Schmidt became only the third National League player ever to win back-to-back MVP honors when he hit .316 and again led the league in home runs.

Truly, here is a player of heroic proportions, the stuff of legends, a sure-fire Hall of Famer. Signing such a big-name talent would seem to have been easy, like picking choice fruit from a strong vine.

But Tony Lucadello tells a different story. It's a tale of patience — long, long years of it. And hope — tons and tons of it. It's a story of great secrecy and, ultimately, great reward.

I signed Mike Schmidt to his first major league contract in June of 1971. The fact that I signed him wasn't so surprising. Mike was a definite prospect. Twice he'd been All-American for Bobby Wren's Ohio University Bobcats. He'd helped the team win Mid-American Conference championships three straight years (1969–71) and set a slew of records in the process.

But what few people know is that landing Mike Schmidt wasn't accomplished in one season, or two, or three. Getting Mike Schmidt's name on a contract culminated six long years of some of the most intense scouting I have ever had to do. Secrecy was the main thing, and during those six years I doubt Mike even knew I was interested in him.

Scouting hadn't always been that way, like a cloak-and-dagger spy game. But the draft changed everything. Before the draft, I'd go the other way around the house. I'd knock on the back door, meet the family and get buddy-buddy like, and hope they liked me enough to influence their boy to sign with my team.

Then the draft came along in 1965 and everything changed. Suddenly, a ballplayer could be drafted by any team, starting with the last-place club on up. You could be thinking you'd found the next Mickey Mantle but it wouldn't be worth a plug nickel if another team drafted him ahead of you, then signed him.

That's why I had to develop a cloak-and-dagger secrecy to my scouting. The less other scouts knew about my feelings toward a ballplayer, the better chance I had of signing him. I feel I have a pretty good reputation of signing some excellent ballplayers, but if I showed my face every time he stepped onto a ball diamond I could lose a promising young prospect. If another scout found out I had a boy high on my list, all he'd have to do is raise the boy just as high on his list and, if his team drafted ahead of us, they'd swipe him right away.

At times I've held up reports to my office so no one would know exactly how high I was on a player. Other times I'd deliberately make a fuss over a player I wasn't really interested in just to throw other scouts off the track. Maybe part of my success in signing guys like Toby Harrah, Todd Cruz, Tom Underwood, Barry Bonnell, and Jim Essian is because I never exploited the fact that I wanted to sign them. Sometimes it's frustrating and often I think about how it was in the old days, but that's how it's done now. It was a tough transition to make at first, but I never believed that crap about old dogs and new tricks anyway.

Mike Schmidt was a budding prodigy in this era of the draft. I liked him the first time I saw him back in the spring of 1965. One of my part-time scouts, Ed French, had called to say there were a couple of talented sophomores I should come take a look at. Both played for Dayton Fairview High School, a catcher named Ron Neff and an infielder named Mike Schmidt.

So I went down to check out the boys, and at first glance I could see that Schmidt was an excellent athlete, and a better than average prospect. I felt, though, that Mike would be a late bloomer. At times he did things that truly amazed me; other times he did not play well. But that was in my favor, I thought, because it might leave doubts in the minds of other scouts. I had this feeling about Mike (you get these feelings when you've been scouting as long as I have and you learn to trust them) that somewhere down the road he was going to develop into one fine ballplayer. It was just a matter of time.

Now that I'd found a prospect, I planned my strategy. Knowing that other scouts would be checking on my whereabouts, secrecy was my greatest concern. I saw Mike just once more his sophomore year, but I made it a point to see him play several times before he graduated. Always I remained incognito, hiding behind the other team's dugout, or a bush or tree near the field. I watched one game from the back end of a station wagon out in the parking lot and another time, when I got to the ballpark and saw a few scouts already there, I never even bothered to stop.

In no way did I want to tip my hand. I never contacted Mike, or Jack and Lois Schmidt, his parents, or his high school coaches, Dave Palsgrove and Bob Galvin. I stayed away from everyone even remotely close to Mike for fear that somehow word would leak out that I was interested in signing him. Even when Mike graduated high school and was eligible to sign, I stayed away. I still did not feel he was quite ready.

I wasn't worried about Mike's development as a ballplayer. He was involved with what I consider two of the finest programs in that part of the state: Bobby Wren at Ohio University, one of the best college coaches in the game, and Ted Mills in Dayton, who runs some of the top amateur teams in the country.

An astute baseball man, Bobby Wren made some pivotal changes in Mike, including changing Mike from a switch-hitter to more of a power hitter when he noticed Mike seemed more comfortable from the right side of the plate. Bobby and I were good friends. He'd always been honest with me, so I confided in him and told him I wanted to sign Mike. Bobby knew my position. He knew I was a target for other scouts and he knew the game I played. He knew how I worked and how I operated. Whenever I went to Athens to see Mike play college ball I always called Bobby and we'd discuss Mike's progress. And in the four years Mike was at OU, Bobby never tipped my hand.

A legend on the Dayton amateur baseball scene, Ted Mills's Parkmoor Restaurants team won the 1967 national championship and six times since 1976 has won the Dayton Class AA title, considered one of the finest amateur leagues in the Midwest. Mills's 1971 Cassis Packaging Company team also won a national championship. In eighteen years of coaching, Mills has won nearly 700 amateur games.

A standout pitcher himself before a freak accident ended his career, Ted Mills has pumped money from his own pocket into the amateur programs. Ted just wants to make sure young prospects have a chance to play ball, and that's how his path crossed Mike Schmidt's.

Ted Mills caught Mike at a crossroads. An eighteen-year-old just out of his freshman year of college, Mike needed direction and a chance to prove himself. I have said that I thought Mike was a late bloomer. I felt all he needed was a bat, a glove, and a chance to play and he'd come through. And Ted Mills supplied the opportunity that set Mike on the right path.

The way Ted tells it, though, the seeds that would blossom into Mike Schmidt's future were not so neatly sown. Ted had seen Mike play at Fairview High, but wasn't greatly interested in the young infielder. Ted saw Mike several more times in the summer of 1967, when his Parkmoor Restaurants team was rolling toward a national title, but still wasn't impressed enough to ask Mike to join his AA team.

A year didn't change matters much. Mike hit only about .260 for OU's freshman team. He had just one home run and wasn't spectacular in the field. Summer came, and again Mike was not invited to join Parkmoor's club. However, though no one knew it at the time, the scales of fate were about to take a decided dip in Mike's favor.

Dayton's Tom Smith played for Bobby Wren at OU and Ted Mills wanted him for his Parkmoor team. During their conversation about Smith, Wren told Mills that he might consider picking up another player of his, Mike Schmidt.

When Mike still had not heard anything by early summer, his father, Jack, and Lefty Baker approached Mills and asked if there was room on the team for Mike. Mills said his roster was full, but that another team in the AA league might be looking for players. So Mike checked out the rest of the league, but I think he had his heart set on playing for Parkmoor.

Later the same day, while Parkmoor was playing Lafayette, Indiana, in a doubleheader, Mike approached Mills himself and asked to join the team. Either out of frustration or pity, Mills put Mike in the game. Filling in at second in the nightcap, Mike popped up and flied to center in two times up. It was an inauspicious beginning, but that would soon change.

Though not formally with the team, Mike kept showing up for practice. That gritty determination, inherited from his parents and fortified by Mike's greatest fan, his grandmother, finally earned Mike a spot on the roster and, eventually, a starting position. The more Mike played the better he got. Mills got a glimpse of Mike's budding power when, in one practice, he ripped four consecutive pitches over the softball diamond that sits beyond the leftfield fence at Princeton Park. All blasts were well over 400 feet. But the move that proved Mike had made it came in midseason when Mills replaced Mike Leffel, his starting shortstop who was hitting .375, with Schmidt. Ted Mills had made his choice, and in the process set in motion the wheels of a great future.

At first, Mike struggled as he adjusted to the starting lineup. He had his 0-fer days and his share of strikeouts. But confidence was growing in Mike, and with that confidence came consistency. In late July, for example, Mike belted four homers and a triple in one three-game outburst. By season's end Mike led both the Dayton AA League and the Indiana League in home runs. Despite his slow start, Mike hit a respectable .271 in the Dayton League and a sparkling .304 in the Indiana circuit. The Mike Schmidt that would one day earn back-to-back MVP honors was gradually taking form.

Another cornerstone of Mike's future was laid in the summer of '68 when Rich McKinney was drafted by the Chicago White Sox. McKinney, who also played in the Dayton AA League, just happened to be OU's starting shortstop. His absence opened a timely opportunity for Mike. Mike stepped in admirably, earning all-MAC honors the next few years and setting records for everything from home runs to total bases and walks.

Mike spent his sophomore and junior summers in the Illinois Collegiate League, another fine amateur division. Mike was with Peoria in 1969 and the following year he led the league in homers and walks and topped all shortstops in fielding, assists, and doubleplays while with Springfield. Mike capped his college career with another all-American performance, then started the summer of '71 with Ted Mills's Cassis Packaging Company team.

Throughout this time I had been the "Invisible Baseball Scout" as far as Mike was concerned. I did talk to him a time or two when he attended my camps in Richmond, Indiana, but I kept the conversations instructional. We talked about his hitting and fielding, not contracts. My real scouting was still done in hiding as I lurked behind bushes and trees and anything handy.

I still maintained that my secrecy would give me a better chance of signing Mike. Some scouts, I knew, were leery of Mike's knees, since he'd had operations on both while in high school. But I knew Mike had worked on a strict weight program in college, lifting twenty pounds, then forty, then sixty, until his knees were as good as ever. I was hoping to use that fact to bluff a few other scouts, but in the race to sign Mike Schmidt, the finish was closer than I expected.

Ted Mills had written the California Angels about Mike, and Walt Day, a scout with Minnesota, was interested. And, though Mills and I both pushed for Mike to be drafted No. 1, neither of us succeeded. We drafted a pitcher in the first round and so did the Angels, a boy named Frank Tanana. In Mike's first all-star game, ironically, the first pitcher he faced was Tanana. I believe the Angels had Mike as their number-two choice, but fortunately we drafted ahead of them in the second round. I'd finally landed Mike Schmidt, and six long years of back alley, cloak-and-dagger scouting were rewarded.

I called Mike shortly after the draft and we set up an appointment. We met — Mike, his dad, and I — at the North Holiday Inn in Dayton. I made an offer; Mike asked for a bit more. Mike was shy, but he was straightforward and honest and knew what he wanted.

Right then I picked up the phone and called Paul Owens, our farm director.

"What do you say, Paul? Can I give him the extra money?"

"Sure," he said. "We want him."

It was as quick and simple as that; one of my easiest signings, really. There were no hassles, no arguments, no quibbling over details. It was cards-on-the-table time and we both got what we wanted.

Mike started out at Reading in the Eastern League, but hit just .211 and only had eight homers. Despite those numbers, Mike moved up to AAA ball the following season and was outstanding. In 131 games at Eugene, Oregon, Mike hit .291, blasted 26 home runs, and had 87 RBI. He was brought up to Philadelphia at the end of the season, but got into just seven games.

Mike opened the next season with the Phillies, but 1973 was as awful as 1972 had been awesome. Mike hit 18 homers and drove in 52 runs, but his average dropped to a dismal .196. He struck out 136 times in 367 at bats.

Suddenly, I was catching a little heat from the front office. Here I had bragged a ballplayer up as a number-one draft choice and he wasn't even hitting his weight. Mike's slump, though, followed a pattern I had seen throughout his career. Mike had struggled on Ted Mills's team then came on strong; he struggled his first year in the pros, then had that great year at the AAA level; he was struggling now, but I knew he would come on. I never lost that feeling that somewhere, somehow, Mike Schmidt would come through.

"Just hang with him," I said. "Sooner or later Mike Schmidt will find himself."

Mike did, exactly one year later. Mike won his first home run title the following season, belting 36 round-trippers to go with a .282 average and 116 RBI. When he led the league in homers the next two years and hit 38 again in 1977, it only solidified Mike's position as one of the great power hitters in the game. A 45-home run total in 1979 seemed the ultimate, but then came the classic 1980 season — 48 homers, 121 RBI, a .286 average, and National League and World Series MVP honors.

The joy I get from scouting is seeing a player reach the major leagues through hard work and determination. But when a man accomplishes what Mike Schmidt has, I'm simply astounded.

My one regret is that, because of the way I had to scout Mike

Schmidt, I didn't have a chance to get to know him and his family on a close, personal basis. That was the biggest advantage the old style of scouting had over the cloak-and-dagger system one has to use these days.

That's the way I am, though. I feel that if a player has made it to the big leagues, he has enough to think about without me stopping by all the time. If I'm the scout that signed — and my name is on the contract of all the ballplayers I've signed — I'm happy with that. If I'm in Chicago or Cincinnati or Pittsburgh and a player I've signed is in town, I don't feel it's my place to be out at the ballpark or down in the locker room pumping his hand. I don't believe in that. He's in the big leagues; he has his own people. He has a job to do and probably more than enough people bugging him to death for tickets or autographs or whatever. He doesn't need me hanging around.

Besides, I have work of my own to do. There just might be another Mike Schmidt out there somewhere, and I want to be the guy who finds him.

More Than Just a Job:
The Signing of Fergie Jenkins

◆ ———————————————— ◆

Big money contracts. High-priced trades. Too bloody often baseball breaks down into a numbers game of dollar signs and decimal points. And the substance and character of a man can be overshadowed by his batting average, his ERA, or the number of figures in his contract.

It's mercenary in a sense, but true. A fact of the trade is that success in the major leagues is measured by statistics — hits and home runs, wins and ERAs, and, yes, even dollars and cents. Once in a great while, though, a moment of the sport transcends the cold hardness of facts and figures. One man, a scout, becomes more than just a hunter of raw talent. Another man, a prospect, becomes more than just a product.

Consider Lucadello's signing of Fergie Jenkins, a transaction that went beyond the limitations of facts and figures and made the business of scouting more than just a job.

I will be greatly surprised if, someday, Fergie Jenkins is not inducted into baseball's Hall of Fame. In the late '60s and throughout the '70s, Fergie Jenkins has consistently been one of the game's most durable pitchers: nineteen years in the big leagues, over 3,000 strikeouts, almost 300 wins. When the Chicago Cubs signed Fergie in 1982 they were just hoping that, at thirty-nine, he could be a steadying influence on their younger pitchers. He ended up leading the team with a 14–15 record and 3.15 ERA.

I was with the Philadelphia Phillies when I signed Fergie back in 1962. We traded him to Chicago early in his career, though, and his greatness will historically always be linked with the Cubs. That was one reason I was happy to see the Cubs pick him up again.

Another reason is the closeness I have for Fergie and his family. It's becoming a rare thing in baseball, but a genuine friendship developed between Fergie, his family, and me. It was an amazing thing, and it all started long before I'd even heard of Ferguson Arthur Jenkins.

Back in the early '50s, when I was still covering a good portion of the Midwest for the Cubs, I heard about a promising young shortstop named Gene Dziadura. He was from Windsor up in Canada, but Casey Lopata, our Michigan scout, had seen him play in Detroit. There was no real organized baseball in Canada at the time, so the Canadian boys who wanted to play the game crossed the river and played on the sandlots of Detroit. That's where Casey first saw Gene Dziadura, and that's where I first saw him. It wasn't long afterwards that I signed him to a Cubs contract.

Gene was an excellent prospect. He was a good fielder and hit well, but what sold me was his instinct about the game. He just looked and acted like a big leaguer.

Unfortunately, Gene never had a chance to make it. Seemingly destined for the major leagues, Gene injured his back in an accident, and his hopes for a pro career ended suddenly.

Gene, though, was a gutsy young man. Determined to make the most of his life, he returned to Canada, earned a college degree, and became a teacher in Chatham, Ontario. It was characteristic of Gene that he would choose teaching, a job where he could work with young people. And, though no one could have foreseen it at the time, one of the youngsters who would come under the influence of Gene Dziadura was Fergie Jenkins.

When I began scouting for Philadelphia in 1957, I covered basically the same territory I had covered with the Cubs. I needed part-time scouts, though, especially in Michigan and the untapped areas of Canada. Gene Dziadura was the natural choice, and when I asked him if he wanted the job he jumped at the chance.

So Gene kept his mind on teaching and his eyes on any talent in the area. Baseball, naturally, wasn't the main sport in Canada. Hockey was. Serious fans around Chatham and Windsor might follow the Tigers, who were just across the river in Detroit and all, but there wasn't the degree of interest as there is in Michigan and the States. I suppose now that Toronto and Montreal have major league teams the interest has grown tremendously, but back then baseball was just something done to pass time in the summer. Pickup games on back sandlots were about all there was because most high schools and colleges didn't even offer the sport.

Canada had many outstanding young athletes, though, and it was one such standout who eventually caught Gene Dziadura's eye.

"How about coming up and checking the boy out?" he asked me over the phone. "I think I got a real prospect."

So, with the help of Casey Lopata, we set up a tryout camp in Chatham (probably one of the first held in Canada) and asked Gene to bring the boy along. It was there that I got my first glimpse of Fergie Jenkins. Just fifteen then, Fergie was six-feet-three-inches and all of 155 pounds of budding potential. Hockey was his major interest at the time, naturally, but his talents extended beyond the ice arena. In his high school career, Fergie lettered in hockey, basketball, soccer, track, and golf. Three times he was voted most valuable player on the basketball team and, as a senior, he was named athlete of the year.

Despite Fergie's inexperience in baseball, he showed great promise at the first tryout camp. A natural athlete, he displayed excellent velocity and surprising accuracy. Though rough in his fundamentals, Casey was as impressed with the boy as I. Here, certainly, was potential worth keeping an eye on. That job fell to Gene Dziadura, who, having been denied a shot at professional baseball himself, did all he could to help another reach that goal. Occasionally, I'd slip up to Chatham to visit Fergie and his family, just to check on his progress, offer a bit of advice, and keep in close contact with them.

Much of the credit for Fergie's development, though, belongs to Gene Dziadura. Year after year, through the long winter months, Gene taught Fergie the mechanics of throwing a baseball and the basics of pitching. Each time I visited up north I saw a little more polish on that diamond in the rough.

Gene even helped us turn one of Fergie's favorite pastimes into an exercise to build up that long, lean frame of his. Fergie loved hunting and even raised his own German shorthair hounds. His real passion, though, was just being out in the woods, out there mixing with nature. When we learned that, we devised a little scheme. Often, on the many, many times we visited the Jenkins family, we'd send Fergie off into the woods with an ax and tell him to whale away at any old stumps and trees he could find.

"The kindling's gettin' kinda low, Fergie," we would say. "Better go chop some firewood." Sure enough, he'd get a big grin on his face and off he'd go. I can't remember how many ax handles we had to replace, but Fergie will tell you it was quite a few. Damned if it didn't pay off too. Swinging that ax all winter and a sledgehammer in summer (an idea Gene added), Fergie developed the wrist, forearm, and shoulder strength that I feel made him such a durable pitcher. Back then we didn't have the extensive weight programs and exercise equipment they have now, but we figured old-fashioned hard work would be the best thing for him. It was.

Leo Durocher seemed to think so too. Durocher liked big, strong, durable pitchers, and Fergie fit the bill. In Fergie's first seven years with the Cubs, he led the National League three times in starts and four times in complete games. He was traded to Texas in 1974, but ended up leading the American League with twenty-five wins. Until Fergie was thirty-six years old, he averaged something like thirty-six starts a year. And the amazing thing is that when the Cubs got him back in '82, he started thirty-four games at the age of thirty-nine. Now that's durability, and I like to think Gene Dziadura, Casey Lopata, and I helped develop the strength and talent that has allowed Fergie Jenkins to continue in his career when players younger than him are falling away.

Now back to how I signed Fergie in the first place.

Fergie graduated from Chatham Vocational School in June of 1962. Until he graduated he could not be signed to a professional contract. As his graduation neared, though, I grew more and more apprehensive. Our organization wanted him badly, but several other teams had also found out about Fergie and were just as interested. Remember, this was back at a time when every player was basically a free agent and could negotiate with any team he pleased. Other teams, I knew, had been trying to wine and dine the Jenkins family and get close to them. As the contract deadline approached, I worried more and more about my chances of signing Fergie.

But a rare thing had happened in my relationship with these

people. A relationship based on business — an interest in their son as a major league baseball player — developed into a genuine friendship. I did not realize how close we had become until I actually signed Fergie.

I had met Fergie's parents during that first tryout camp in Chatham. His father, a chef at one of the finest hotels in Chatham, had always been open, straightforward, and supportive. His mother, a remarkable woman, was almost blind. She had an amazing sixth sense about her, though. I could knock on the door and she'd say, "Come on in, Tony." Or I could call and before I could say it was me she'd ask, "Tony, how've you been?" It was uncanny.

As I said, several other teams were interested in Fergie's services. But because of our relationship, his parents would not allow him to talk with any other club or negotiate with any other scouts. They just made up their minds that regardless of the money and regardless of what anybody else had in mind, Fergie was going to sign with the Phillies. In all my years of scouting they are the only family I've known to take such a determined, active stand in the signing of their son. I realized then the magnitude of the friendship that had grown between us, a realization Fergie reiterated to me several years later in a letter.

"Even though it was a time when scouts felt they had to wine and dine a family to get their kid's name on a contract, that was never the case with us," he wrote. "Mom and Dad loved to have you visit, not because you were after my name on a dotted line, but because there was a genuine interest between us. They knew you were interested in me not only as a ballplayer, but as a human being. They respected that, and that is why we became such good friends."

The actual signing of Fergie Jenkins was almost anticlimactic, but no less an example of this great friendship. And, ironically, I ended up the one wined and dined.

Shortly after Fergie graduated high school, his father fixed a magnificent meal, complete with candlelight and more trimmings than a Thanksgiving feast. After we ate, we talked — like friends getting together for a chat — about what we planned for Fergie, about the offer I had in mind (a very good offer, I might add), and about his future. Midnight came, and shortly thereafter Fergie Jenkins put his name on a professional baseball contract.

Fergie spent his first week as a pro ballplayer at Williamsport, Pennsylvania, with our Class A club, then was assigned to Miami in the Class D league. But this was a man destined for greatness, and his rise was meteoric. After a 7–2 start at Miami, in which he struck out sixty-nine batters in sixty-five innings and posted a 0.97 ERA, Fergie jumped to Class AAA ball with Buffalo in the International League. Just one year later, he was in the major leagues.

The sports pages have followed Fergie's progress since then. But what the sports pages seldom show is the beginning, when the unselfish devotion of Gene Dziadura gave another young man the chance he never had, and when two people opened their home and their hearts to this little baseball scout from Fostoria.

Dick Drott

◆————————————————◆

Tony Lucadello's signing of Dick Drott may have been the most all-encompassing transaction of his career. In this case, the mere placing of a young man's name on a dotted line epitomized the entirety of scouting. Involved in this contract were key contacts, dedication, determination, reward and, yes, even the greed, emotion, and luck that make scouting such a fragile occupation.

Joe Hawk is a legend in his own time. He must be eighty or so but he's still going strong, still managing Cincinnati's Bentley Post American Legion team. He's been doing it for years, forty-five or fifty it seems. Joe's won five national championships and turned out a bundle of great ballplayers. That's why I liked to keep in touch with the kingpin of Cincinnati's amateur baseball program.

Late in the '50s, when I was still with the Cubs, I was down checking out Joe's club. They were playing a team from Lawrenceburg, Indiana, and just kicking the crap out of them.

I could have left after a few innings. I'd seen enough. But I had heard a lot of good things about a young boy named Dick Drott and, with a big lead, I was hoping Joe would put him in the game. One inning passed, then another, and still I didn't see the boy. As I went to get a drink of water between the eighth and ninth innings, I figured I had missed my chance.

28

One of Bentley Post's ballplayers reached the water fountain about the same time as I and I waved him to go ahead. Only when I'd finished and noticed the boy still standing there did I recognize him as the ballplayer I'd heard so much about — Dick Drott.

"You a major league scout?" he asked. And when I told him yes he blurted out, "Geez, you're the first scout I've ever talked to. Can I have one of your cards?" I gave him one, naturally, but our conversation ended there. His team was taking the field and sure enough he was going to pitch. Dick Drott faced three batters that inning and struck out all three. He was only about fifteen at the time, but I was impressed.

From that point on I kept in touch with the boy. Often I'd write, and when I was in town I'd call him and drop over to see him and his parents. We all developed a close relationship.

That relationship continued right up through high school, when Dick could sign a contract. By then, though, I wasn't the only dog in the hunt. Dick had gotten better and better and several clubs were interested in him. Between his junior and senior year, a lot of teams that played in Cincinnati had given him a tryout and many of the major league managers had said they were willing to put up a lot of money to get him. The demand for his services was so great that, on the day following his graduation, Dick Drott's father had set up a timetable for major league scouts to come in and make their offers.

Because of my relationship with Dick Drott and his family, I asked when I should come by. It was Dick himself who said I should come over the night he graduated. He wanted to see me first.

I got to their house about eight that night. There wasn't much I could do since he couldn't sign until after midnight, but we talked about the Cubs and the organization as a whole.

When I mentioned we planned to offer Dick $4,000, though, I thought Dick's father was going to fly through the roof. "I can't believe it," he said. "We've known you. We have for a long time. But we've always been honest with each other and I don't mind telling you some teams have offered as much as $100,000. We have to consider the money angle, Tony, and all I can say is that $4,000 isn't enough."

The $4,000 figure, though, was my limit — and with good reason. There was a major league rule in effect that year, a rule that seemed to fluctuate from one year to the next, that stated if a ball-player signed for more than $4,000 he had to remain on the major league roster for two years. If he signed for $4,000 or less, he could be assigned to any of a team's farm clubs. It might seem like a silly rule, but it kept the rich ballclubs from buying up all the best ball-players so they could dominate the standings year after year.

I could only offer $4,000 because our organization didn't be-lieve in offering huge contracts. It was ridiculous to keep a player, especially a young, untested player, on the major league roster for two years when he should be honing his skills in the minor leagues. A quality ballplayer had to learn the trade first, then come up through the ranks like all but a very choice few do.

But our organization's philosophy wasn't the issue just then. Money was. Round and round the argument circled, Dick's father talking about the money and the appointments lined up for the next day and me saying I could offer just so much and, again, explaining why.

Dick's mother, I could see, was quite upset by the whole or-deal. I knew she wanted Dick to sign with me. I knew Dick himself wanted to sign with me, and I felt the father felt the same way. But I couldn't really blame them. The $100,000 was a tremendous offer and I couldn't ask them to turn it down. I was too close to them to ask them to do that.

Just when I thought my chances were being sucked down the drain, though, Dick spoke up.

"Mom . . . Dad," he began tentatively. "You always told me this was my decision to make. I'm the one who's gonna have to play. It's my future . . . and my decision. I've already made up my mind. I'm signing with Tony. I'm signing with the Cubs because I really believe I ought to go through the farm system. I don't want to go to the big leagues just to throw batting practice for two years. I wouldn't accomplish anything and I'd probably get sent down anyway for lack of experience."

The father, a bit shaken by his son's statement, again brought up the issue of money. He was, naturally, concerned about the fi-nancial well-being of his son.

Dick, though, was a determined young man. And his mind was made up.

"We're not wealthy people," he said, his voice taking on a tone of confidence. "But we're not broke either. We'll get along fine. I expect to make it to the major leagues, but I want to make it the right way. I want to be a major leaguer, but I won't be one if all I do is take up space on some club's roster for two years.

"I want to sign with Tony and I want to do it tonight. I don't want all the hassle with the other scouts. That's a problem you created, not me. I didn't set up all the appointments or ask for any offers.

"Tony's the first scout who recognized my talent. He's stood behind me and worked with me. He's talked baseball with me for four years, and I feel I should sign with him. That means more to me than all the money in the world."

The finality of the young man's words took us all by surprise. The father stopped his incessant pacing and the mother, stunned by the torment between husband and son, wiped her tear-stained face and sat up on the couch. It was just after midnight.

"Honey," the mother said, dabbing at her eyes. "In our hearts you know we wanted Tony to have our boy. All we are thinking of is the money. Dick's right. It is his decision and he knows what direction he should take. We owe him that opportunity. That way he'll know he earned his way to the top."

As I glanced over at Dick's father I saw his shoulders droop, perhaps in supplication, perhaps in relief. He consented to my offer and, about 1:30 in the morning, I signed Dick Drott for $4,000.

With orange juice and coffee we celebrated, if a celebration it could be called. When I got up to leave they asked for advice on how to handle all the scouts that were anxiously awaiting their turn. "Say that he's already signed with the Cubs," I told them. "Tell them the truth. It's always the best way."

We sent Dick Drott to Cedar Rapids, Iowa, and he had a good year with their Class B club. He spent the following season in Los Angeles, then jumped to the majors. In his first year with the Cubs, Dick Drott won fifteen games on a last-place team. I thought that was one of the most amazing things I've ever seen a young man do in three short years. But Dick Drott had that kind of talent, and that great belief in himself. Even in that living room of his parents' house you could feel that self-confidence showing through.

I had come to expect that from Joe Hawk-coached players, though. The young men Joe picked from Cincinnati's Elder and Western Hills High School grew to be more than just athletes under his tutelage.

Jim Brosnan, another Bentley Post pitcher I signed, is a prime example. Brosnan didn't get the nickname "The Professor" for nothing. A bright young man, Brosnan once interviewed me on a team bus, wrote an article, and sold it to some publication. After nine years in the big leagues, Jim Brosnan became an accomplished author.

For the pure test of scouting, though, I don't believe anything can top my signing of Dick Drott. It was so amazing, in fact, that it damned-near got me into trouble with the head man himself, baseball commissioner Happy Chandler.

You see, when the other scouts heard I'd signed Dick Drott for $4,000 they couldn't believe it, not when they had offered as much as $100,000. Nobody could possibly turn down that much money.

Claiming something had to be rotten in Denmark, they reported me to Chandler. The commissioner called me in and quizzed me on the situation. I told him exactly what happened, but I don't think he really believed me. They investigated my bank records, they investigated my neighbors, they investigated everybody associated with the signing to determine whether I had given the boy a lot of money or not. Even Dick Drott, his parents, and his parents' bank records were investigated. All summer long I was hounded.

"I don't know how much longer I'm going to take this," I finally told Jack Sheehan, our farm director. "They don't believe me. They're still hounding me, and I can't see when it's going to get cleared up. I think it's time someone told P. K. Wrigley the story."

It wasn't long before I got a call from P. K. Wrigley himself. "Tell me the story, Tony," he said, and I did.

"Mr. Wrigley," I told him, "if I gave that boy more than $4,000 you'd be the first to know. Nobody could know quicker than you because it's your money."

P. K. Wrigley knew nothing underhanded had gone on. No money had passed under the table. So he contacted Happy Chandler and explained the whole deal. It wasn't long before the commissioner made everyone drop everything real quick. All the accusations vanished, and that ended it.

It was disconcerting, though, to realize some people put dollar signs ahead of friendship and devotion.

Grant Jackson

◆————————————————————◆

Tony Lucadello observed thousands of young ballplayers in his many years as a major league scout. Many of them didn't have the impressive high school and amateur statistics of a Mike Schmidt, Larry Hisle, or Alex Johnson, but they did possess the natural raw talent a man like Lucadello could unearth in a boy.

Players like Toby Harrah and Larry Cox were, as the title of this book indicates, diamonds in the rough. Lucadello may have had to knock a little dirt off here and smooth over a few rough spots there, but underneath he knew there was a major league ballplayer.

It was the same way with Grant Jackson, a gem of a ballplayer Lucadello discovered and polished to perfection right in his own backyard.

I once knew a man in Fostoria, Ohio, a quiet, gentle sort of fellow, who loved baseball. For hours we would talk about this team or that team, the tested veterans and the promising rookies. It was a love of the sport he instilled in his son, Grant Jackson.

Grant's father knew I was a major league scout. He also wanted his son to be a ballplayer, so it was only natural that he would get us together.

He called me one day, a day way back in the '50s, and asked me to meet him out at the ballpark. "Come take a look at my boy, my pride and joy," he said. So I threw a few balls in the car, picked up a glove, and headed on over.

Grant was only about nine at the time, but don't get the impression I was out there playing patty-cake with a little kid. Grant's mechanics, naturally, were very crude. But even at that young age he showed me a good arm. He was strong, he had good velocity on the ball and, most importantly, he seemed eager to learn. You can improve the mechanics of a young ballplayer, but you can't give him natural talent.

I decided to keep an eye on this young Grant Jackson, especially when his father passed away a few years later. It was terribly unfortunate that the man who had sparked Grant's interest in baseball would never get to see the fulfillment of that dream.

I didn't know if I'd get to see that fulfillment myself, not back then anyway. You see, Fostoria didn't have a high school baseball team, and Grant had nowhere to get a start in organized ball. Fortunately, there came along a man of interest and insight, though. His name was Andy Veres and he operated a sporting goods store. Andy had two boys who also wanted to play some baseball but had nowhere to go. So Andy organized an American Legion team and fitted it out.

For two years Grant played on the team, learning more and more all the time and getting better and better. I saw several of his games and kept constantly in touch. Occasionally, I'd offer a tip or a bit of advice. And to help his progress I invited Grant to our tryout camps every summer. They were held in Gomer. Ed Sandy, a former big league pitcher, and two of my part-time scouts, Casey Lopata and Pete Mihalic, always helped out. They were impressed with Grant's speed and velocity, but all agreed he needed more work.

When Grant graduated from high school there was a question as to just what he would do. He said he was going to college, though, because that was what his mom wanted.

Grant's mother — I really respect that woman. Every time I'd see her she'd have a big, hearty smile on her face. She was a strong woman who ran her family with a strong hand. I admired the way she handled her kids. They all had to try and be the best they possibly could be, and that usually meant going to college. Grant was no exception.

Grant enrolled in Bowling Green State University that fall,

but things didn't work out. He transferred to a branch campus, but that didn't help.

Grant called me then, and said college just wasn't for him. He said if he was going to make it anywhere it would have to be on a baseball field and wanted to know if I was still interested. I said I was and that I'd keep in touch.

This was one of those cases where I had to sell our organization on a ballplayer, not the other way around. When I called our front office, I told them I wanted to sign a kid who deserved a chance. I said he didn't have great mechanics, but that he had a good strong arm and I'd personally work with him to improve his technique. That must have sold them. I got the OK and signed Grant for the following season.

The contract was signed, sealed, and delivered, but the real work was just beginning. Grant still needed a lot of training. And with the fall of 1961 turning into a chilly winter, the outlook was bleak.

Another man stepped forward, though, to continue a legacy born of a father's love of baseball and nurtured by Andy Veres's development through the American Legion program. The man was John McMillan, the director of Fostoria's YMCA. John said he'd help any way he could and offered us the use of the YMCA basement whenever we wanted. Given a path to our goal, Grant and I went to work.

Five days a week for almost five months the YMCA basement was like a second home. Grant threw thousands of pitches against that cold concrete wall, and every single pitch made him that much better. Afterwards he'd lift weights to increase his upper body strength. On and on it went, day after day. Pitch and lift, pitch and lift. Gain the technique, then magnify it with strength.

Grant made steady progress, but as spring came on I became worried that I had gotten too close to the boy. Maybe he looked good to me simply because I liked him and had been the only one working closely with him. He needed a test.

I arranged for Grant to pitch to some of the better hitters at Bowling Green State University. I took Grant over and Dick Young, BGSU's coach, lined up the players.

The first batter stepped in real confidently, but was stepping back out a few pitches later. The second did the same thing. Finally, Dick asked me to take Grant off the mound. His hitters, he said, were afraid of his fastball. Grant had passed the test with flying colors.

Grant's next move was Florida and the Instructional League. I expected to hear good things about him, but no word came. His mother hadn't heard anything either and, concerned, asked if I'd find out what was what. My worst fears were put at ease when the assistant farm director told me Grant was one of the best young pitchers in camp. He was doing so well, in fact, that instead of assigning Grant to Jamesville, Wisconsin, where I had expected him to start at the Class D level, they were promoting him to Bakersfield, California, and Class C ball. Grant had been so involved in making the big leagues, it seemed, that he'd forgotten to write home.

The rest of Grant Jackson's story is well documented. He reached the majors in 1967 and has been a standout reliever ever since. He's pitched on six major league teams and been in three World Series.

It was interesting to note that when, at the age of thirty-nine, Grant Jackson was traded from Montreal to Kansas City, Royals' manager Dick Howser said he felt Jackson still had a "live arm." Maybe it was all those pitches against the YMCA wall, the same pitches a boy named Scott Nye is making. Nobody drafted Scott, but I signed him. He needs a little work on mechanics and fundamentals, so we go down to the "Y" and work on it.

Who knows? Maybe I can polish me up another diamond in the rough.

From Hardwood to Hardball:
The Signing of Larry Hisle

◆——————————————◆

In the late 1970s Larry Hisle was acknowledged as one of the premier power hitters in the game. With Minnesota in 1977, Hisle hit .302, ripped 28 home runs, and led the American League with 119 runs batted in. Traded to Milwaukee the following season, Hisle hit .290, knocked in 115 runs, and hammered 34 homers (second highest in the league). Just over thirty and reaching his prime, Hisle was one of the sport's rising superstars.

In the midst of this great career, though, disaster struck. A shoulder injury which developed in 1979 eventually ended a brilliant major league history by the young slugger. Hisle played in just twenty-six games in 1979, seventeen in 1980, and twenty-seven in 1981. Hisle hoped to make a comeback in 1982, the year a powerful Milwaukee team breezed into the World Series. But the recurring shoulder injury never responded to treatment. While his teammates were tearing up the American League, Hisle, who appeared in just nine games, watched from the sidelines. Afraid that any further attempt to play the game might ruin his arm permanently, doctors advised Hisle to give up baseball. In 1983 he hung up his spikes for good.

It was a sad ending to a great player's career. But the fact that Larry Hisle played baseball at all is the real story. As a youngster Hisle didn't like baseball, didn't like the game at all. Basketball was his sport, and the NBA his goal. How he went from pounding the hardwood to pounding the baseball is a tale worth telling.

Mention the names Kareem Abdul-Jabbar, Larry Bird, and Moses Malone and you think of one sport — basketball. Mention the name Larry Hisle and automatically baseball pops into mind. But few people know that if Larry Hisle hadn't signed a professional baseball contract, he probably would have seen more fastbreaks than fastballs in his athletic career.

Larry Hisle was an outstanding basketball player at Portsmouth High School. Twice he was named all-Ohio and, his senior year, he was selected a prep all-American. Over a hundred colleges recruited him heavily. He visited several, often in the company of another sought-after player, a tall kid named Lew Alcinder. The Big "O" himself, Oscar Robertson, tried to get Hisle to attend Cincinnati.

But I'm a baseball scout, not a college basketball recruiter. I'm interested in guys wearing spikes and ball gloves, not short pants and sneakers. So I didn't know much about Larry Hisle until Harry Weinbrecht, the Portsmouth head coach and a part-time scout of mine, asked me to check out a player of his. You might have heard of him; his name is Al Oliver and he's done pretty well in major league baseball himself.

I went to Portsmouth to scout Al Oliver, but quickly turned my attention on Larry Hisle. You couldn't miss him. Big and strong, Larry was a natural athlete. He had speed, agility, power, strength — all the tools, as they say in the business. I learned Larry's first love was basketball, but as I delved into his background I came across an interesting history.

Larry's mother died when he was rather young, and his father, I heard, was an invalid. The people who mostly raised Larry were Orrville and Cathalee Ferguson. Cathalee was a cousin of Larry's mother, and after her death the Fergusons took Larry in. I don't know if they formally adopted him, but Larry always referred to them as his mom and dad and said it was the environment that they gave that made him a success later in life.

The Fergusons were true baseball fans, especially Cathalee. If it hadn't been for her, Larry Hisle may never have gotten into baseball in the first place. Basketball was his sport and he was going to make it a year-round project. But Cathalee said there were enough hours in the day to play both sports and that he should at least give baseball a chance. She loved baseball and couldn't understand why a talented young athlete wouldn't want to be on the field every day.

Larry was a bit of a conniver, though. After he asked if he could quit playing baseball and was told no, he came up with a plan. He figured that if he screwed up in practice, the coach would cut him and he'd be free to go play basketball. But the plan was never put into action. Larry's background and training wouldn't allow him to do it. The Fergusons taught Larry that it's not important what you do, as long as you do it to the best of your ability. The important thing was never to cheat yourself.

So when Larry walked out onto the baseball field, the competitive juices started flowing and the desire to excel took over. He knew that to demand less than the best he could offer was to expect in return less than he could possibly achieve, and he wouldn't allow that to happen. If it ever did, he realized he'd be hurting Orrville and Cathalee Ferguson more than himself. I noted that characteristic of Larry's often in my scouting reports.

Instead of trying to get out of baseball, Larry began to excel at it. His ability was obvious, but Larry also had an advantage in that he worked harder than many players with equal or greater talent. You wouldn't think a guy with his natural talent would have to, but that's what often separates a major leaguer from just another ballplayer.

It probably didn't hurt that Larry was surrounded by some pretty darn good talent, especially in American Legion play. In addition to Larry in the outfield and Al Oliver at first, Gene Tenace played shortstop for the Portsmouth Post 501 American Legion team that was awesome between Larry's junior and senior year of high school. They won the state championship that season, and in one of the tournament games Larry did something I have rarely ever seen. Portsmouth was playing in Athens on the varsity diamond of Ohio University, a major league size field. Larry put three home runs out of the park, one to left that bounced off the gymnasium, one to center, and a third to right. I once saw Alex Johnson put three out in one game for me, but Larry's awesome display of power was like nothing I had ever witnessed. About the only thing I can compare it to is Mike Schmidt's four home runs in the opening game of the 1976 season.

Already very high on Larry, I hoped to sign him after he graduated from high school. But there were other teams interested in Larry, too, and I knew we'd have to draft him high. Basketball, though, beat us all to the punch.

"Larry," I said once when I called to find out how he was doing, "how'd you like to play professional baseball?"

"Sorry," he said. "I'm going to college. I've accepted a basketball scholarship from Ohio State."

It was a setback for me, but I was determined to keep trying.

"Well, would you mind if we at least drafted you?" I asked.

"You can," Larry said. "But I think you're wasting a draft choice."

We drafted Larry Hisle in the second round anyway, but I couldn't get him to sign. At the time, Larry was at a crossroads of two sports, basketball and baseball, and he was taking the path he felt was best for him. Larry attended orientation and worked out with Ohio State's basketball team. His collegiate career — in basketball — seemed certain.

Suddenly, everything did a complete turnabout. I won't go into the details surrounding the incidents that changed Larry Hisle's direction from college basketball to professional baseball. I will only say that I feel pressure was put on Larry to attend Ohio State, and when the nature of that pressure came to light Larry was allowed to turn down the basketball scholarship, leave school (he later returned on his own and earned his degree), and sign a professional baseball contract.

Whatever the reason, I now had a ballplayer to sign. And I knew I had to give it my best shot.

I had kept in touch with Larry continually and now I called him with what I hoped would be the clincher.

"We'd like you to play for the Phillies," I said. "If I brought the team's owner, general manager, and farm director down here to talk to you, do you think you would sign with us?"

Larry was still undecided about his future. "It might be a wasted trip," he said. "But you're welcome to come."

I set up a meeting at a Holiday Inn in Portsmouth, and Robert Carpenter, Paul Owens, and John Quinn came down from our front office. Larry, with his stepfather and stepbrother, met us there. We made Larry an excellent offer and signed him easily. I found out why later.

"When you called the other day, it was the first time in my life

I seriously considered a career in professional baseball," Larry told me after signing. "I made my mind up on the way over and I knew it was the right thing. I figure that if the owner of a major league team would come all the way down here to convince me to play ball, you people in the game must know more about my ability than me."

Larry Hisle made Cathalee Ferguson proud. And Cathalee Ferguson is as proud of Larry Hisle the ballplayer as she is Larry Hisle the person.

"I'm not a psychologist or philosopher, but I truly believe people are a product of their environment," Larry once told me. "I know everything I've accomplished is due to the experience and training my stepparents instilled in me. They taught me how to cope with life, and that lesson has paid off twice.

"The first time was when my mother died. That was the most tragic moment of my life. I knew nothing could ever hurt me as much. But I survived, and the experience prepared me for any situation. The roto-cuff injury that ended my career tested me, though. The constant pain coupled with the disappointment and inability to compete was almost too much. It was close, real close, to the first experience."

Tag-a-Long:
The Signing of Toby Harrah

◆————————————————◆

Ever been to a garage sale and found the perfect little lamp you have been looking for to set off that one bare corner of the den? It's just what that room needs and you have to have it. But when you go to buy it you find out it's part of a matched set. And not only do you not need the other one, you don't even like it. A chip's missing from the base, the shade is faded, and the cord's all frazzled and worn. If you want the one, though, you've got to buy the other. What the hell do you do?

You can forget the lamp, though you may not find another like it. Or you can go ahead and buy both, and be stuck with one old lamp you cannot use.

It's a dilemma similar to the one Tony Lucadello faced once. But he was dealing in people, not lamps, and the stakes were a lot higher.

I never sign a young ballplayer to a major league contract unless I feel he can play professional ball. My purpose as a scout isn't just to find good athletes, but to find the type of athlete that will be a productive asset to our club. I have to admit, though, that I once made an exception. I signed a boy I knew didn't have an icecube's chance in Hades of making the major leagues. Here's how it came about.

LaRue, Ohio, is a small town six or seven miles west of Marion. The kids in that area go to Elgin High School. American

League umpire Larry Barnett graduated from there, and in the mid-to-late '60s the school had some fine athletes. Not the least of them was Toby Harrah.

Toby was born in Sissonville, West Virginia, but his family later moved to Ohio and settled in Marion. He probably would have attended Marion Harding High and might have gotten lost in the numbers game of the bigger school, but his family moved to LaRue and into the Elgin School District. It was a smaller school, but it gave Toby the opportunity to develop and excel. Emil Rubcich was his high school coach then, and it might be best here to let him describe Toby's prep career:

"Toby was one of only two or three four-sport athletes we've ever had at Elgin. And I'm not positive, but he might be the only one ever to be all-North Central Conference in all four sports in the same year. Toby quarterbacked us to the football championship his senior year, throwing fifteen or twenty times a game with no interceptions the entire season. He was the leading scorer in basketball, he was a shortstop on the undefeated baseball team, and he was a long jumper and high jumper in track.

"Toby wasn't that big, maybe five-foot-nine and 155 pounds. But he was an excellent athlete and he could excel at a smaller school like Elgin. Toby had a great attitude. He was polite and pleasant and 'sirred' all the coaches. He did all a coach could ask and led by example.

"Toby could be ornery, though, and he sure liked the gals. He came from a large family. Good stock and street-fighter tough. I found that out one day in gym class. As phys-ed teacher I was always trying new things in gym, and one day I decided we'd do a little boxing. This was during the basketball season and Toby just happened to be in the gym shooting around. One kid kept egging Toby to go a few rounds with him, but Toby just shrugged him off. He had nothing to prove. After ten or fifteen minutes of razzing, though, Toby had had enough. He just said, 'All right, let's go,' put on a pair of gloves, and hammered the kid ten or twelve times before I stepped in to stop it. He was a scrapper.

"Toby's toughness was especially evident on the baseball field. He wasn't a pitcher, but I put him in now and then when we were in a jam. I only pitched him an inning or two at a time, but he didn't allow a single hit his whole senior year. All told, it would have been a ten- or twelve-inning no-hitter.

"Toby was an outstanding baseball player at Elgin, but it was a boy named Scott Fields that drew the attention of scouts like Tony Lucadello."

That's for sure. Most of the scouts in the Midwest had heard of the big six-foot-five lefthander from Elgin. I had been to see the boy pitch several times and there always seemed to be a bevy of scouts around.

The more I saw of Elgin, though, the more impressed I was with the team's little shortstop, a boy named Toby Harrah. He didn't get much of a sniff from the other scouts, but he caught my eye. I could see the boy had good speed and an excellent arm. He had good movement and nice hands. What impressed me most, though, was the way he handled himself on the field — always confident, always in control.

As Elgin's season drew to a close and with the draft not far off, I had a little talk with Toby. I asked him if he was interested in professional baseball. He said no. He was going to college, to Ohio Northern University, to play football, basketball, and baseball.

I was interested in signing Toby, but not interested enough to come up with the kind of money that would pay for a college education. Besides, I figured if he wanted to play football and basketball that much, he wasn't ready to concentrate on baseball. I didn't press the issue.

The draft came and Fields was selected by the Tigers. He went to Ohio University and played for Bobby Wren, but he never made it to the major leagues. Hurt in an accident, he never had the chance.

Toby, meanwhile, played American Legion ball with Lima right after high school. I saw quite a few of his games and talked to him often. I hoped to change his mind by telling him that three sports was a lot to be involved in during college and that he'd really have to bear down to keep his grades up and remain eligible. But he said he could handle it. He was going to Ohio Northern, and he was going to play football, basketball, and baseball.

I didn't push Toby after that. I went about my business, scouting all parts of the Midwest. And Toby played for the Lima Legion up until the team was eliminated from tournament play.

The summer passed and September came. And as I do every September I pulled out my card file of prospects and started calling around. Sometimes young men change their minds about college and decide not to go. And if they're not in college, I'd rather have them playing ball for us than just sitting around.

Eventually, I got around to calling the Harrah house and Toby's mother answered. Toby had gone to orientation and worked out with the football team at Ohio Northern, she said, but he had returned home and was working in Marion. I left a message for Toby to call me and a few days later he did. It was getting on in September, but summer was still holding on and the weather remained warm and sunny.

I asked Toby if he had changed his mind about pro ball and he said he had. So we set up a workout the following Sunday at Findlay High School. Toby came over and brought a friend. I didn't know who he was, but he shagged flies and helped with the workout so I didn't mind. I just figured he was one of Toby's buddies.

I worked Toby out at the Findlay diamond for three straight Sundays, and his friend always tagged along. After the third week I was ready to offer Toby a contract, but that's when things got a little sticky. Toby said he'd sign, but only if I signed his buddy too. Both or none. That's the way it was going to be.

I thought Toby was kidding me, so I played along with the joke for a while. His friend didn't appear to be a bad athlete, but there was no way I could project him as a major league ballplayer. The material — and the potential — just weren't there.

I kept trying to sign Toby, figuring he'd put his signature on the contract anytime. But I soon learned he was serious. If our organization wanted Toby Harrah, we had to take Toby Harrah's friend too. Take it or leave it.

My negotiations with Toby stretched well into the winter. December passed and we made no headway. January was likewise cold, bleak, and fruitless. By mid-February I was getting desperate. Spring training wasn't far off. If Toby wanted to be there, he'd have to sign soon. As a last resort I called Paul Owens, our farm director then, and explained the situation.

"I don't know if you'll like this idea, Paul" I said, "but why don't we sign his buddy too? We were thinking about giving Toby $1,000 to sign, so why don't we split it and give each $500? Then we get them both down to spring training and after Toby meets some other players and gets settled we'll see what happens. We're going to have to keep an eye on his buddy so he doesn't get hurt, and naturally we'll have to let him go eventually. He just doesn't have the ability to play major league ball."

Surprisingly, Paul Owens agreed, and a day or two later I was back in LaRue signing two ballplayers, Toby and his tag-a-long friend.

Toby and his buddy went off to spring training, but it wasn't long before I got a call from Ruly Carpenter, who was down in Florida learning the business so he could one day take over for his father as president of the club.

"Tony," he says, "I can't believe what I'm seeing down here. There's a boy on one of the rosters who you signed, and we paid good money to, who couldn't play on a lot of high school teams. What's going on here?"

I asked the boy's name, but knew it was Tag-a-Long before he answered.

"Uh, have you talked to Paul Owens, Mr. Carpenter? He'll tell you the story."

"I want to hear it from you, Lucadello. What gives?"

So I explained the situation in detail, mentioning how Tag-a-Long came in a two-for-one deal to get Toby Harrah.

"Wait a minute, Tony," Mr. Carpenter said. "We're not so sure about this Harrah kid, either. He's got some ability, but he hasn't shown us anything outstanding yet."

That got me a little riled. I'd worked long and hard to sign Toby Harrah and I wouldn't have gone after him if I didn't think he was major league stuff.

"Let's talk about Toby Harrah," I said. "I know you check a players' speed in the sixty-yard dash. How'd he do?"

"Fine," Mr. Carpenter said. "He has good speed."

"And I know you put 'em behind third and have 'em throw to first to test their arms. How's that?"

"Good. He has a good, strong arm."

"Well, then, what about his hands, and his fielding?"

"He's a good defensive player. He handles himself real well."

"Then it must be his bat."

"Yeah, that's it," Mr. Carpenter said. "There are fifteen guys down here who don't think he'll be able to hit major league pitching."

"He's only been there a week," I said. "How can you know so soon whether he'll hit or not? If those other fifteen guys know so much you should make them all scouts and you'd have the best staff in baseball. Toby Harrah could be another Clarence Jones, a boy I once signed out of Newark. He got out of the naval reserves just in time for spring training, but he wasn't given a chance. He got released, but another team picked him up a day later and he ended up playing eight years for the Cubs.

"Give Harrah a chance. Let him play a while and you'll find out he's a pretty good ballplayer. I judge a prospect on four things — speed, a good arm, how he handles himself defensively, and hitting. You've said he meets three of the four qualifications. Heck, we've signed players with only one or two plusses and they've made it. Give him a chance. The hitting will take care of itself."

We kept Toby Harrah, but not his buddy. Unfortunately, Toby never played for the Phillies. I'd have liked that. We lost him to the Washington Senators early in his career. Toby played minor league ball in Huron, South Dakota, under Joe Lonnett, now with the Pirates. Joe really liked Toby, but he had a feeling we were going to lose him. There was a policy in baseball back then that if you didn't protect a player in your organization, other clubs could place him at a higher level in their system, if they had room for him. If you put a player at the AAA level, for example, another club could "draft" him and put him on their major league roster. A player at the AA level could be claimed by another organization's AAA team, and so on.

Joe had heard of at least six teams that were interested in Toby, so to protect him totally we would have to put him on the major league roster. We only bumped him to the AAA level, though, and sure enough Washington got him away from us. It might have been for the best. In a little over a year Tony had gone from high school ball to the major leagues. That was back in 1969, and Toby's been in the big leagues ever since. As a matter of fact, he might be the only active player who played on the Senators' last team in Washington (1971). A year later they were the Texas Rangers, and that's where Toby really blossomed. Overcoming some early problems, like an illness in 1972, a broken finger in 1973, and the instability of being shuffled between short and third, Toby developed into one of the top third basemen in the game. Even after being traded to Cleveland, a perennial sixth-place team, in 1979, Toby kept producing: .279 with 20 home runs that first year with the Indians, .291 in 1981, and his best year, .304 with 25 homers and 78 runs batted in in 1982.

I always felt Toby was big-league caliber, even when he was just a little guy playing for Elgin High School. I always say: they don't stay five-foot-eight and 145 pounds forever. Sometimes those small packages are hiding a big-league ballplayer inside.

And, though I don't like to rub it in, I did get a bit of satisfaction from the scouts who missed out on Toby Harrah. I was in Cleveland, ironically, shortly after spring training for an awards ceremony of some sort. Toby was doing well and his name was getting around.

As I entered the lobby of the hotel I saw ten or twelve other scouts, and they came rushing over. "Who's this Toby Harrah?" they asked. "Where's he from and how did you find him?"

I recognized some scouts who had been to Elgin to see Scott Fields, so I spoke to them.

"How many times did you see the Fields boy from Elgin pitch?" I asked, and they said at least ten. "Every time you saw him you saw Toby Harrah. He was the shortstop on that team."

"You signed that little guy?" they laughed. "They'll knock the bat right outta his hands."

"You just keep thinking that way," I said. "When Toby Harrah's up in the big leagues and you're out here scrounging around for a bit of talent, you remember this: You don't measure a major leaguer by the size of his body; you measure him by the size of his heart."

Tools of Genius:
The Signing of Larry Cox

◆————————————————◆

It's a simple plaque with a simple message. But it was one of Tony Lucadello's most prized possessions. On it is written:

TO
TONY
THE BEST SCOUT
IN O.B.
(organized baseball)

The plaque isn't from the Chicago Cubs organization, nor the Philadelphia Phillies, though Tony sent enough major leaguers to both clubs to warrant the honor.

The plaque isn't from Mike Schmidt either, or Fergie Jenkins or Toby Harrah or Larry Hisle or any of the big-name players Tony has signed. The name under the inscription belongs to Larry Cox, and if you haven't heard of him don't feel too bad. In baseball's shining galaxy Larry Cox was anything but its brightest star. His career totals after eight years in the majors — 182 hits, 12 home runs, 85 runs batted in, and a .208 average — would not add up to one good season for many of today's top players. The only time Larry Cox was considered a first-string player was when he caught about 100 games a season for Seattle in 1979 and 1980.

But Larry Cox is a survivor, one of those junkyard-dog type players who scrap and claw and work their way up the hard way. It hasn't been easy. Cox labored nine years in the minor leagues, switching back and forth eighteen times between eleven different teams, including the Phillies. Now managing in the Cubs organization, Cox's background reads like a Rand-McNally road-map — four different major league teams, ten minor league clubs, winter ball in Culiacan, Mexico, and twenty-five relocations in nineteen years in professional baseball.

Larry Cox, though, epitomizes the type of ballplayer Lucadello had great success in signing, the kind of player who reaches the major leagues not because of God-given talent or ability, but the kind who makes it through desire and determination.

I love telling the story behind Larry Cox because he was a young man who never gave up. He could have, many times and for many reasons. Minor leaguers don't make that much money, and with a wife and three kids I know it was tough sometimes. But Betty, his wife, was a real pioneer of a woman. Larry was shuffled around quite a bit in the minors, but every time he was reassigned she'd pack up the car and the kids and follow wherever he was sent. They were a close family, and I think that closeness got them through the rough times.

I'm happy that I signed Larry Cox, but I have to admit I got kind of lucky too. Larry was one of those players I just stumbled across.

Larry was an excellent ballplayer at Ottawa High School, one of the bigger schools in Putnam County up in northwestern Ohio. He was Putnam County League MVP a couple of years, I guess, and even drew the interest of a few scouts when he was playing on the Ottawa American Legion team that went to the state tournament in '64. But I hadn't seen him play or scouted him. I actually ran across him by accident.

I had a friend in Fostoria, and his son played baseball. He was a pitcher, and a darn good one by what his father said. Week after week he hounded me to see his boy pitch. I'd certainly be impressed, he said, and would probably want to offer him a contract. But something better always seemed to come up, and I was always going in the opposite direction when his boy was pitching.

I tactfully avoided a confrontation until late August. One night I received a call from my friend (if he still considered me one after that summer) saying his boy was pitching the next night against Ottawa in a Legion makeup game. Couldn't I go scout his boy? It was the last game of the season, and probably my last chance to see him.

Well, there really wasn't much going on at the time. I was pretty well done with scouting for the season, and Ottawa wasn't far to drive to see one last game. So I said I'd take a look at his boy in action, and a day later I was on my way to Ottawa.

I got to the ballpark around seven, got the lineups for both teams and, since there were no other scouts around, settled up in the stands. It was still early, but there was a good crowd on hand and pretty soon I was in a friendly conversation with several people in my area. Naturally, we talked baseball and they told me about a fine young catcher for Ottawa, a boy named Larry Cox. I checked the lineup and was surprised to see Larry Cox playing second, but they insisted he was a better catcher and was just filling in one game at second.

To tell you the truth, I don't remember who won the game. The Cox boy didn't do a bad job at second, and my friend's kid didn't do too bad of a job on the mound. But I wasn't that impressed with either one of them, not as major league prospects anyway. I jotted their names down on filing cards but didn't plan on signing either one.

Two months passed and I forgot about Larry Cox. But I came across his name one day while leafing through my files and it stuck with me. I had listed him as a catcher on the information the fans had given me, though I'd never seen him catch. I noted that he didn't have good size for a catcher, but that he had an excellent arm and handled himself well on the diamond. I was about to put the card back when I figured what the heck. It was a slow time for me, the boy didn't live far away, and I could afford to at least go back and check him out, this time as a catcher.

I went to Ottawa soon after and located the Cox homestead. His family (and it was a big one with ten or eleven kids) lived in a large farmhouse just outside of town. Larry's father worked for Ford in Lima and his mother, a jolly and likable woman, ran the house. I met her first, since Larry was working, and we sat in the kitchen and talked while she prepared dinner.

It was during that first visit that I got an indicator of what kind of athletes they had in the family. While the mother cooked, the young ones raced around the house. One of them, a daredevil of about five, pulled some of the most amazing stunts I'd ever seen.

Up and down the hall he ran, turning cartwheels and tumbling and bouncing into everything. Every once in a while he'd race into the kitchen, jump on the table, and do a backflip onto the floor. Then he'd laugh, race down the hall and back into the kitchen, and do it all over again.

I mentioned something to the mother but she paid no mind. The kids were just showing off for my sake, she said, and I should just ignore them. It scared the dickens out of me.

Larry came home a short time later and the first thing I noticed was his size. He had put on some weight and his job at a lumber company had really muscled him up. Physically, he looked much better than I remembered.

We sat and talked and I told Larry it was unfair of me to judge him as a catcher when I'd only seen him play as an infielder.

"I'd rather catch," he said. "That's always been my best position."

"All I can do, Larry," I said, "is try you out and give you a chance. If you want to try professional baseball I feel you have to go as a catcher. What I'd like to do is work with you for a few months. Findlay has a brand new YMCA and I know the director over there. His son, John Poff, has played some minor league ball. They have a driving range in the basement where golfers can practice in the winter, but if I talk to the director maybe he'll let us use it during their slack hours. We'll work on your catching, your throwing, your hitting — all the fundamentals. What do you say? You want to give it a shot?"

"You bet," Larry said, and I could see by his reaction that enthusiasm was one thing he would never lack.

We started the following week working out three nights a week at the Findlay YMCA. Tom Lawrence, who was from Findlay and who had signed with the Phillies organization, worked out too. We had to make some adjustments, using tennis balls instead of baseballs and broomsticks instead of bats, but it paid off. The more I saw of Larry Cox the more I felt he could make it to the majors.

I signed Larry to a contract early in 1966. We had one final tryout, this time over at Bowling Green State University against a pretty decent pitcher. It was a cold, windy day and I even had to go out and shag a few flies, but Larry looked good and he went to spring training.

Larry began his minor league career with Huron, South Dakota. Joe Lonnett was managing the team, and I think he helped Larry a lot. Larry Hisle was up there too. Larry only hit .219, but he was never known as a great hitter. Larry's greatest asset was his defense. He had a great arm — they even tried to make him a pitcher one year — and he really knew how to call a game. I think that's why he was so valuable with the Cubs in '78, Seattle in '79 and '80, and Texas in '81. Those teams all had young pitching staffs and I think they were looking for a catcher like Larry, a great defensive catcher with a lot of experience and savvy who could handle the young hurlers.

Larry displayed his great defensive abilities right from the start, as I quickly found out. After a year at Huron, Larry was sent to Spartansburg, North Carolina, a minor league club in the Western Carolinas League. One night I got a call from Robert Carpenter, who owned the team then. He had an estate in Spartansburg and when he vacationed there he liked to go out and see the team play.

"Tony," he said. "Did you sign a young catcher, a boy named Larry Cox?"

"Yes, sir," I said. "I believe he's at Spartansburg right now."

"Tell me, Tony," Mr. Carpenter said. "What did you sign him for?"

"I don't know what his salary is now," I answered, "but we signed him for a $500 bonus."

"Is that all?"

"Yes, sir. Why, did I do something wrong?"

"No, Tony," he said. "You just might have gotten us one of the biggest bargains ever. I saw him play last night and he did something I've never seen before. He picked three men off three different bases in the same inning.

"It was the fifth or sixth inning and his team was up by a run. The other team seemed to have a rally going when the first guy led off with a triple, but Cox picked him off third. The next guy singled, and Cox picked him off too. The third batter walked and took second on a wild pitch, but Cox picked him off to end the inning. I don't know if that's ever been done in a baseball game before. It could be a first. Boy, that kid's got a gun for an arm.

"Tony, I just wanted to call and say congratulations. The boy may not hit much, but with his defense and great arm I know you've signed yourself another major leaguer."

I had, but it would take another seven years before Larry Cox would become a full-fledged major league player. We did call him up in 1973, but he only appeared in one game. It was a year later that he would play thirty games for the Phillies, bat .170, and send me the plaque. It's something I'll treasure always. I'm as proud of Larry Cox as I am of Mike Schmidt, Fergie Jenkins, Larry Hisle, or any of the other players who've made it in the big leagues, because Larry Cox made it the hard way, through desire, determination, and dedication.

They say a catcher wears the tools of ignorance. I beg to differ. Larry Cox will be an asset to a team, probably in a managerial role. In his case, tools of genius seems more appropriate.

The Waiting Game:
The Signing of Tom Underwood

◆———————————◆

Like Kenny Rogers sang in his hit single "The Gambler," sometimes you just have to know when to hold 'em and when to fold 'em. Baseball, like poker, is often a game of patience. You don't tip your hand, but neither do you rush blindly into a hand before all the cards are on the table.

Tony Lucadello learned that lesson early in his scouting career, and many times that bit of knowledge paid off. It certainly did in the pursuit and signing of Tom Underwood.

Mothers know. They always do, you know. They have that inner sense that lets them know when you're being honest with them or just throwing them a snow job. When I first started scouting, I learned that in a hurry. A baseball scout has to be honest with people and honest with himself. And if he sticks to that guideline, whether it hurts sometimes or not, he builds a good reputation as a scout. That reputation, sooner or later down the line, may one day land him a ballplayer. In the case of Tom Underwood, I feel it did.

The pivotal point in the signing of Tom Underwood came late in the summer of 1972, when he was pitching for Bob Ronk and the Kokomo (Indiana) American Legion team. The beginning of the story, though, went back much farther.

One of my scouts, Ed French, first recommended Tom Underwood. But since Ed was down in Hamilton, Ohio, and Underwood was up in Kokomo, Indiana, I assigned my Indiana man, Norm Kramer, to check up on the boy. Norm saw Tom and his first report was favorable. Underwood wasn't overpowering, Norm said, but he had an excellent curve and good control. That was good enough for me, so with Norm's report in hand I decided to have a look-see myself. I went to see Tom Underwood the following week and almost tore the report up. Not overpowering! All the kid did was strike out nineteen batters, blowing the ball right by all of them.

This was a mystery. Norm's report said one thing, but I'd seen something entirely different. I had to have another look. I was also getting desperate, because the June draft was only a week away and I had to be sure of this Underwood boy.

A week later, the day before the draft, I was back in Kokomo. Kokomo High was in tournament at the time, Tom pitched, and he was unbelievable, allowing only a hit or two and striking out twenty-four in ten innings. It was an awesome performance and I was impressed. I knew then we had to get the boy, but time was short. I had to contact my office and let them know how high I wanted Tom Underwood drafted. I didn't feel they would go for number one, but I knew we had to draft him at least in the second round. Any lower and I was afraid another club would steal him away.

As soon as I got back to my motel I phoned Dallas Green in New York. When Paul Owens became general manager a week or two before, Dallas had been moved up from assistant farm director to director of minor leagues and scouts, and it was through him I'd had to deal. I explained to him how Tom Underwood had an average major league fastball, but with a tail on it, as most lefthanders have. His curveball was outstanding, I said, and he had excellent location with all his pitches. The key, though, was that the boy *knew* how to pitch.

"Mr. Green," I said, "he's a definite prospect in my mind. I predict he'll be in the major leagues in two years. If we want a shot at him, I don't think we can afford to draft him any lower than the second round."

Dallas said he'd see what he could do, and that ended the conversation. I had gone out on a limb for Tom Underwood. I wasn't known for last-minute phone calls telling the organization who to draft and where. I had put my reputation up as collateral but it must have been worth something. The next day we drafted Tom Underwood in the second round.

Drafted, though, doesn't mean signed. Tom was still under high school eligibility, since his team was still in the tournament, and we couldn't sign him until that eligibility was used up.

In the meantime, another interesting development sprang up. My glowing report on Tom Underwood had the front office buzzing and had piqued the interest of team owner Ruly Carpenter himself. They must have thought I'd found the next Walter Johnson.

Now I consider Ruly Carpenter and his father Robert two of the best owners the game has seen. Knowledgeable and dedicated men, they took an interest in baseball at all levels. Robert Carpenter was there when I signed Larry Hisle, and Ruly was showing the same determination as his father. Still, I was a bit surprised when he suggested he and Dallas Green come down to check out this young phenom I'd cost them a second-round draft pick over.

I told Mr. Carpenter when Tom would be pitching next and we made arrangements. When Ruly Carpenter and Dallas Green flew into Indianapolis, I picked them up and drove them over to Anderson, where the tournament was being held. We got to the ballpark and I introduced Mr. Carpenter and Dallas to Tom's parents. Since Tom's father John Underwood had played in the Phillies' organization, there was plenty of common ground for conversation and we got along real fine.

Tom pitched a pretty fair game, though he wasn't as overpowering as I'd seen him earlier. Kokomo won 1-0 and struck out 14, but I could tell Mr. Carpenter wasn't all that impressed. It was like he'd come to see Nolan Ryan and got Ryan O'Neal instead. But, he said, he still wasn't sure, and if he could arrange it he'd like another look at the boy. We set it up for the following Saturday when Kokomo would be playing its next round of the tournament.

Again Mr. Carpenter and Dallas flew into Indianapolis and again I picked them up and took them to the game. It was almost a mirror image of the first game. Kokomo again won 1-0 and Tom again fanned thirteen or fourteen batters. He wasn't awesome, but he got the win.

I had been keeping an eye on Mr. Carpenter throughout the game, hoping to gauge his thoughts by his reactions. But he was impassive, hardly moving until the final out of the game. Then he shocked us all by racing onto the field and going right up to Tom Underwood. For five or six minutes they talked by themselves. Then they shook hands and went their separate ways.

Later, as we drove back to the airport, there was a tense silence in the car. Dallas was driving, as he often liked to do when he came down, and I was alone in the back. I sensed neither of us wanted to open the conversation, but it was Ruly Carpenter who broke the ice.

"Tony," he said to me, "I want that boy under contract as soon as possible. Sign him as quick as you can."

I knew Dallas had liked Tom right from the start. And I was obviously impressed with him or I would never have recommended him so highly. But we were both a bit taken aback by what we felt was a sudden shift in Mr. Carpenter's outlook.

"Why the change of heart, Ruly?" Dallas asked. "You weren't that impressed with the boy last week and he certainly didn't show you anything else today."

"Well, I'll tell you," Mr. Carpenter said, leaning back in the seat and cracking a grin. "I had a little talk with the boy, as you two no doubt noticed. And it was something he said that made up my mind.

"I asked the boy if he was tired, and he said no. I asked if his arm was sore and again he said no. Then I asked if he realized he hadn't pitched any better today than he had last week, and he said he was aware of that. So I asked him if he thought he could throw harder than he had, and he said he was sure he could. Then I asked him why he didn't, and you know what he said? He looked me square in the eye and said, 'Mr. Carpenter, I always thought that to be a good pitcher you have to go out there on that mound, whether you have your good stuff or not, and win a ball game. I didn't have my good stuff today. But if I can beat a good team without it, they're certainly not going to beat me when I have it.'

"That really impressed me. I've never heard anything like that before, especially from someone so young. When he said that I knew this kid had what it takes. Tony, you sign him."

Holy mackerel! I felt like I'd gone from the outhouse to the penthouse in a fast elevator. Earlier I'd felt that I had cost the club a choice number-two draft pick; now I rejoiced that everything had worked out all right. It was a happy crew that drove back to Indianapolis, and one happy baseball scout who saw Mr. Carpenter and Dallas Green off on the plane.

Everyone's great expectations didn't last long, though. It would be a long time yet before Tom Underwood would put his signature on a professional baseball contract. It wasn't because of a lack of effort on my part. As soon as Tom's team was eliminated from the tournament, I visited him and his family and made an excellent offer. Tom, though, spoke up.

"We appreciate all you've done," he said. "But my father and I feel I should wait awhile. We feel I should play some college ball before I decide to try the major leagues."

I could have forced the issue, but I didn't. A young man's future in professional baseball often depends on his mental attitude when he makes the commitment. If he feels he's not ready for such a jump, it's not a good idea to push him. You run the risk of losing him altogether.

I had to play the cards the way I felt was best. And that was to ease off, stay cool, and hope something would break in my favor. I told the front office what was going on, then settled back for a long waiting game. Besides, I knew there were extenuating circumstances. I knew Tom wanted to play Legion ball that summer, and I really couldn't blame him. They had a fine team, especially with Tom and his brother Pat, later drafted by Detroit, doing the pitching. And they couldn't have been in better hands than Bob Ronk's.

Bob Ronk is almost a legend in the Midwest as far as American Legion ball goes. He's a dedicated coach and runs a good ship. Scouts always follow his teams because he always has something to offer. He teaches good fundamentals, good baseball sense, and a good knowledge of the game. Though Tom Underwood wasn't in our system, Bob Ronk's was just about the next best thing.

I stayed pretty much out of the picture that summer. I didn't keep bugging Tom or his parents. I knew his mother wanted him to sign, wanted it badly. Mothers know. I only had the best interest of Tom at heart and she sensed that. Not that it made a lot of difference after June 30. That's when American Legion eligibility took effect and bound Tom as tightly as his high school eligibility had earlier.

I didn't chase after Tom, but I kept a constant eye on him. I saw him pitch quite a few times, but he rarely knew I was there. That's why I was so surprised one night to get a call from him. It was late August and Ronk's American Legion team was in a regional tournament in Richmond. Tom asked if I'd come talk to him and, with a pretty good idea of what he had in mind, I headed for Richmond.

I checked into the same motel Tom's team was staying at and located him near the pool out back. We went back to my room and sat down.

"You still interested in signing me?" he asked right off the bat.

I told him I was.

"Then why haven't you been around all summer? You haven't called, you haven't stopped by, nothing."

I explained that there was no point in it, not with him involved in his Legion team and the eligibility rule. I said I'd seen him play several times, though he didn't know it, and told him that I thought he needed the time to make up his own mind about professional baseball. It seemed he had come to a decision.

"I'm glad you're still interested," he said, "because I don't think we're going to last much longer in the tournament. I'm tired. I've pitched a lot of ball this year and, though I won tonight, I don't think we have the depth to go all the way. We already have one loss. One more and we're out. If we get beat tomorrow, we're going to pack up and head home. Will you follow us?"

The long wait was about over. I said I would.

The team lost the next day and was eliminated from the tournament. Tom and his parents loaded up the car and headed back for Kokomo, with me close behind. It was about one in the morning when we reached their place, and in the wee hours of the new day I signed Tom Underwood to a contract.

Everything worked out for the best. And just as I predicted, Tom made it to the majors in just two years. After being named the best lefthanded pitcher in the Western Carolinas League in 1973 and an all-star in the Eastern League in 1974, the Phillies called him up. Tom was 14–13 his first full year in the majors and 10–5 his second. We traded him in 1977, but he went on to have some good years with St. Louis, Toronto, New York (Yankees), and Oakland.

Things worked out well on my end too. Not only did I sign a top pitcher, but I got a new car out of the deal as a bonus. Right after I signed Tom Underwood I called Ruly Carpenter with the news.

"Tony," he said, "I know you never really liked the company car we gave you, so for signing Tom Underwood we're going to let you get any car you want."

It sure did make those trips between Kokomo and Fostoria a lot easier on the old bones.

Iron-Man:
The Signing of Mike Marshall

◆──────────────◆

Tony Lucadello graded prospects on four major points: speed, arm, hands (defense), and hitting. A plus in all four areas was exceptional; three out of four, excellent; two out of four, workable; and one out of four, well that was taking a chance. But Lucadello made a living out of taking chances, and none may have paid off more than the signing of Mike Marshall.

Signing Mike Marshall reminds me a lot of the signing of Dick Drott. Like Drott, Marshall was a very intelligent, very independent individual. Right from the start he seemed to know exactly where he was going and just what he had to do to get there.

Casey Lopata first saw Mike Marshall at Adrian High School in Michigan. His reports were promising, so I went up to check the boy out. Mike graded out well according to my system. He had a little better than average speed, swung a pretty good bat, and had a genuine feel for the game. Mike's greatest asset was his arm, a real howitzer, but what really sold me on him was his competitiveness. Mike's intelligence was funneled into his game. One way or another, he'd find a way to beat you.

Mike pitched and played shortstop both in high school and for the American Legion team of Meine Busch. A young, slender man, Meine Busch loved baseball and proved to be a great disciplinarian

62

and teacher, despite his young age. Like Mike, he was blunt and straightforward, traits I feel gave both men a mutual respect for each other.

When Mike graduated from Adrian High School in 1960, I went after him. As it turned out, though, getting his name on a contract was as much his idea as mine. I had stayed in close contact with Mike throughout his prep career and had gotten close to his family in the years I'd known them. Since this was before the draft, any team could compete for Mike's services. But when he became eligible Mike made the decision himself. He wanted to play for the Phillies and that was that. There was no difficulty whatsoever. We came to an agreement immediately and Mike got a nice contract.

Once signed, we had to decide how to use Mike to his best potential and our best interests. We had two options. Mike was a good shortstop but also an excellent pitcher. His performance in the Hearst Sandlot Classic at Yankee Stadium right after his senior year didn't swing us one way or the other. In that game Mike entered the game as a reliever and eventually knocked in the winning run.

In the end we assigned Mike as a shortstop. But in my report to the front office I said he should be kept at the position a year or two to determine if that was his best route to the big leagues. I made an emphatic point of adding that if shortstop wasn't his best position, he should be tried out as a pitcher because of his magnificent arm.

For a long time, though, it looked as if our first idea was the best. In his rookie season with Dothan in the Alabama-Florida League, Mike led all shortstops with 196 putouts. The following year with Bakersfield, California, he led the league in assists (420) and chances (589) and was named to the all-star team. A year later, with Magic Valley of the Pioneer League, Mike hit .304 with 14 homers and 76 RBI, proof that he could hit as well as play defense.

But Mike Marshall's legacy in the big leagues would not be as a shortstop. Never called up as an infielder, Mike turned more and more to pitching, where that wonderfully awesome arm of his made him a star. We lost Mike in a trade, but he finally reached the majors with Detroit in 1967 and posted ten saves, not bad for a rookie. Mike played for three teams — Seattle, Houston, and Montreal — in the next two years. Seattle and Montreal tried him as a starter, but it was in 1971 with the Expos that Mike Marshall began his dominance as one of the great ironman relievers the game has known. Mike appeared in sixty-six games and had twenty-three saves that season. The following year he tied Cincinnati's Clay Carroll for the most appearances by a National League pitcher (sixty-five). In 1973, Mike's last year with Montreal, he led the majors in appearances (ninety-two) and the league in saves (thirty-one).

Impressive numbers, but to this point they were just the prelude to the glory. Traded to Los Angeles in 1974, Mike Marshall had a season comparable, on a shorter time scale, to Lou Gehrig's ironman performance of playing in 2,130 consecutive games. Of the Dodgers' 162 regular season games in 1974, Mike appeared in 106 of them, a major league record. Amazingly, Mike also appeared in seven of the Dodgers' nine post-season games — two in the National League playoffs against Pittsburgh and all five World Series games against Oakland.

Mike won the Cy Young Award that year, a rarity for a reliever. More importantly, he ignited a trend that has made the relief pitcher, men like Goose Gossage, Rollie Fingers, and Dan Quisenberry, a more vital cog in the sport.

Mike never matched that tremendous 1974 season again. A rib injury slowed him in 1975 and he was traded the following year. Mike moved around quite a bit after that, but the ironman with the golden arm wasn't done yet. Not by a long shot. At the age of thirty-five, Mike resurfaced in Minnesota and proved he still had some magic left in the old arm. After appearing in fifty-four games and getting twenty-one saves in 1978, Mike came back with another banner season — ninety appearances and a league-leading thirty-two saves.

It was a gamble that Mike, blessed with good ability as a shortstop, would make the major leagues on his arm alone. But that's the chance you take in this game. I was betting Mike was young enough, talented enough, and smart enough to make the switch. Of course, it never hurts to sign a player with a golden arm now and then.

A Little Reverse Psychology:
The Signing of Dave Roberts

◆────────────────◆

Sigmund Freud may have been the father of psychology, but wives, children, and baseball scouts have elevated the science to an artform. At reverse psychology they are especially adept. You know, where they want something badly but they know they won't get it if they come right out and ask for it. So they say they want something else instead, figuring they won't get it but that they'll be offered something else, which just turns out to be what they wanted in the first place all along.

It's a simple ploy, but for ages it's been working. Tony Lucadello made reverse psychology a tool of his trade, and rarely did its success match that of his signing of Dave Roberts, a standout pitcher with San Diego, Houston, and several other major league teams in the '70s.

But the signing of Dave Roberts also involved luck, a commodity every baseball scout would like to bottle and keep in his briefcase for just the right occasion.

When I think about it, I'm still amazed at how I "discovered" Dave Roberts. Actually, I found him by pure blind luck. You don't count on luck in this profession; you just accept it. But when you put in the years and travel the miles I have, you're bound to have a bit of luck once in a while.

I had been doing some scouting in West Virginia back in 1959 and was on my way to Portsmouth, Ohio, to check out some prospects I'd heard about. I remember crossing the Ohio River on the Silver Bridge or Silver Span (the one that fell into the river some time back) and driving into Gallipolis. As I got into town I passed a ball diamond and noticed a game going on. I really wasn't in too big a hurry so I decided to stop and catch a few innings.

I sidled up to a tall fellow watching along the third base fence and checked out the two teams. The first thing I noticed was the home team's pitcher, a tall, skinny lefthander with a whippet delivery. He didn't look too bad.

"Who's the boy on the mound?" I asked the guy next to me.

"Why, that's Dave Roberts," he said. "He's a freshman."

Only a freshman, I thought to myself. This boy might be worth keeping an eye on. I watched a few more innings, but before I left I made sure I filled out a card with some information on Dave Roberts.

Every year I send out a ton of Christmas cards to young players I want to keep in touch with. I made sure I sent one to Dave, just to let him know who I was and who I scouted for. Since I didn't have a home address for Dave I wrote in care of Gallipolis High School. Later, in the spring, I wrote again asking for a baseball schedule, but they never sent one. I wasn't too worried, though. Dave was just a sophomore and I figured I could wait a while yet.

The following Christmas I sent Dave another card, and in the spring I again asked for a schedule. Still I received no response. When I kept writing and the letters started to come back unopened, I began to wonder just what was going on. Almost another year passed and I was still trying to figure out where Dave Roberts had disappeared to when I finally got a letter. It was from Charlie Koterba, the baseball coach at Columbus Central High School, and he said Dave was there playing for his team.

Now, from what I heard, Dave came from a very poor background. His real parents had split up and his mother remarried and moved to Columbus. I guess things weren't much better for him there. I heard the only meal he got each day was the one they served at school. Maybe that's why he always looked so thin when I saw him in high school.

But Dave loved baseball and was out there playing. Someone from Gallipolis must have passed the word that I was trying to locate the boy, and Charlie Koterba got in touch with me. I hadn't seen Dave pitch in over two years, but after scouting a few of his games at Columbus Central I could see that he had gotten better. He'd grown to about six-foot-three and was thin, but he still had that whippet delivery that generated a lot of speed. I was impressed enough to go after him.

Dave had generated considerable interest among some other teams, though, and I knew some other scouts were after him too. I figured I'd have the best shot at getting Dave, though, if I used a little reverse psychology.

There was an outstanding pitcher in the Columbus area at the time, a boy from Dublin. Everybody was crazy about him. So I got crazy about him too. I wined and dined him and his parents; always showed up when he was pitching a big game; and generally let it be known that I thought the boy was the greatest thing to come along since Handy Wipes. The kid was a good pitcher, an excellent pitcher to be exact. But I knew there was going to be a helluva bidding war to get him, and I didn't want any part of that. In my opinion, Dave Roberts was a better pitcher at a better price.

I made a big play for the other boy, or at least I made it look that way. I had a decent reputation by that time and I was hoping my attention toward the boy would influence the other scouts and divert them away from Dave Roberts. It was a bit chancy but sometimes you have to gamble a bit. This time it paid off.

Both boys graduated the same night. But I planned to be at only one graduation party, the one where I hoped I would sign Dave Roberts. I'd set up a meeting with Dave and his mother at my hotel and they showed up around nine o'clock. We discussed the contract and how it could really help Dave improve himself and his life. I made my offer clear and simple and he accepted.

Somewhere on the other side of town, St. Louis was signing the standout from Dublin. But they had been high on him all along and made no bones about it. I was pretty sure they'd get him.

My reverse psychology ploy must have worked. But I hadn't really fooled everybody with my misdirected attention. Later, when I talked to Pittsburgh's scout, I found out he had planned to talk to Dave Roberts the day after I signed him.

I felt Dave Roberts would have been a great asset for our club, but we lost him the same way we lost Toby Harrah. After going something like 9–3 at Spartansburg, we moved Dave up to the AAA level, hoping to protect him. Pittsburgh swiped him away from us, though, and traded him to San Diego. That's where he really got started.

Dave Roberts had some tremendous years in the majors. The best, from his standpoint, would have been 1973, when he was 17–11 with a 2.86 earned run average with Houston. Dave won sixteen games for Detroit in 1976, but he got pushed to the background that season when a bushy-haired kid named Mark "The Bird" Fidrych swept the league and the baseball world by storm.

But I like to favor Dave's 1971 season with the Padres. That's when he and another of my signings, Steve Arlin, combined for twenty-three wins, over a third of the entire total by the whole team. Dave's ERA was 2.10 and Arlin's was 3.47, so I always used to say it was a Cy Young season . . . if they didn't mind sharing it.

Steve Arlin was, by the way, the best college pitcher I ever signed. The only problem, though, was that Steve wanted to be a dentist, and he kept missing spring training so he could go to dental school. Oh well. He was a damn good pitcher; now he's a damn good dentist.

Steve was also one of those backyard finds that makes it easier on my old bones. Obviously, he wasn't as close as Grant Jackson, who really was in my backyard, but he played and grew up in Lima and that was a hop, skip, and jump down I-75. I found Terry Harmon at Toledo DeVilbiss, just fifty miles the other way on I-75. A little farther on, at St. Clair Community College in Huron, Michigan, I scouted out Bill Nahorodny. Terry Harmon was special because he spent ten years with the Phillies as a utility infielder, filling in at second, short, or third whenever we needed him, and it's tough to last that long in the majors as a utility player. Of course, that also made him a more valuable commodity.

As for Bill Nahorodny, well, a lot of scouts probably saw him as a third baseman. But I was a good friend of his coach at St. Clair, Dick Groch, and once during a doubleheader when no other scouts were around, Dick put Bill in to catch. That's where he'd have to play if he wanted to make the majors, and we both knew it.

But at least I always knew where to scout Steve Arlin, Terry Harmon, and Bill Nahorodny. There's nothing more frustrating for a scout than to find a prospect, then have him disappear on you. All you can rely on then is a little luck, like I got when Dave Roberts popped up again, and hope you get a chance to cash in your ticket.

Cruz-ing For a Bruising

◆————————————————————————◆

When the Seattle Mariners traded Todd Cruz to the Baltimore Orioles in late June of 1983, much of the baseball world was stunned. Cruz, at the age of twenty-eight, was considered one of the American League's premier infielders and was coming off his finest major league season — a .230 average and a surprising display of power that included sixteen homers and fifty-seven runs batted in. The last two figures bettered, in one season, Cruz's career totals to that point.

Instead of being the stabilizer on a young Mariners' team, though, Cruz was sent to Baltimore. It all worked out for the best for the intense young man from Detroit, however. Making the conversion from shortstop to third, Cruz gave the Orioles a solid defensive player at the hot corner and helped Baltimore win the World Series. Cruz had just three hits in the series, but one came in the second game when he also scored the winning run, and the other two came in the fifth game when the Orioles clinched the title.

It was a happy prologue to a not-so-happy life for Cruz. Raised in a tough, riotous section of Detroit, Cruz was at the heart of the racial, street-gang atmosphere of the inner city. Many scouts would not even visit his part of town. But Tony Lucadello ventured there, and came away with another of his diamonds in the rough.

We told the coach they were gifts, but we'd really brought the

Louisville Sluggers along — Casey Lopata and I — out of fear, not charity. If need be, they were our protection.

Casey and I were at Western Hills High School to check out a promising young shortstop named Todd Cruz. Casey had told me about the boy when I'd asked about some of the better prospects in the Detroit area.

"He's not only the best prospect in the area," Casey told me, "he's the best prospect in the state, in my opinion."

"I'll be right up," I said. "Let's check him out."

"Uh, that might be tough," Casey said. "He's in a pretty bad part of town and I wouldn't recommend going in there. I don't even go there when it's quiet, and right now it's a powder keg. Some gangs have been causing trouble lately and I don't think it's safe."

But I was determined to see this young star, especially since the draft was coming up and I had to complete my scouting reports for the front office. I got the name of the Western Hills coach from Casey and called him, hoping I could make some arrangement to see Todd Cruz.

"Yeah, we got a game today, but I wouldn't recommend you come see it," the coach told me. "We've had some riots between rival gangs in this neighborhood, and right now it's pretty dangerous for a stranger to be seen around these parts. I'd love for you to see Todd, but at this time I'd have to say no."

I'd run into problems in the past trying to check out a ballplayer, but this was a different type of situation. The coach wanted me to scout the boy; it was a matter of whether extenuating circumstances — like a club over the head — would allow me to or not.

I did have a plan, but it would require double-play precision and a nearsighted hitter's luck. I was willing to gamble.

"Maybe we can work something out," I told the coach. "Now, I really want to see this kid, and with a little of your help we just might be able to pull it off. How's about if we come out there — Casey and I — and you meet us at an exact place at an exact time. You must carry some respect, you're the coach, and if they see us with you they might let us alone. The timing has to be perfect, though. If we're early and you're not there, don't count on us sticking around. Or if we're late and we miss you . . . well we'd be in trouble then too.

"Oh, one other thing. From what I've heard from Casey, I'd

appreciate it if you could get a couple of kids to guard our car. It's a company car, you know, and they'd frown on somebody stripping it in downtown Detroit."

"If you're willing to try it," the coach said, "I'll see what I can do."

That's why a few hours later Casey and I were looking through the backstop at Todd Cruz. The coach met us just as planned.

"These bats are for Todd," we told him, showing off a couple of new Louisville Sluggers. He was about to take them when we added that, if he didn't mind, we'd hold on to them until after the game.

There was no great crowd around when we'd arrived at the ballpark, although Casey and I noticed several kids clumped in gangs around the school buildings. They appeared threatening, like hand grenades waiting for someone to pull the pin.

We were more interested in Todd Cruz, and for a while we kept our attention on him. About the third inning, though, one of the gangs, about twenty boys in all, broke away and headed our way. In seconds they were swarming around us.

Casey and I were tensing up when the coach came rushing over and told the group we were baseball scouts there to see Todd Cruz. He even pointed out that we were nice enough to bring along two new bats for Todd to use. We weren't there to cause trouble, he told them, so they might as well just leave us alone.

The gang backed off, but two innings later they were back, jostling around like wolves over fresh meat. Again the coach came over and explained who we were and asked the boys to move back. Again they retreated.

We weren't bothered the rest of the game, thank God. Afterward, we told the coach we were impressed with Todd and wanted to set up a workout with him. This was a better situation, just Todd and us and at a location we could choose. We held the workout at a park near Dearborn and Todd was tremendous. We were sold.

Now I had to convince our cross-checker, Brandy Davis, that Todd was a top prospect. But that was another problem. Brandy could only be in town certain days, and Todd's remaining games were all scheduled to be held at Western Hills. Luckily, we got two big breaks.

The first was when one of Todd's games was moved to Butchel

Field, which was in a much better section of town, because the visiting team refused to go into the Western Hills area. We got a second break when that team showed up late for the game. With some time to kill we ran Todd through another workout and Brandy, who'd come in to see the game, had a perfect opportunity to see him in action. We were the only scouts there; the rest thought the game was at Western Hills and they didn't go there anyway.

We saw about five innings of the game that day, but that was all it took. We all realized we had a definite prospect. I suggested we make him our number-two pick, and that's where we drafted Todd — second in the 1973 draft.

Now came the hard part. We'd drafted Todd second, but I hadn't met his parents or anything. All I knew was that they were separated. So I called Todd and asked him to meet me at the Fort Shelby Hotel in downtown Detroit. It wasn't far from his home and I was familiar with the place. A lot of umpires stayed there, just as I did when I was covering the American League.

Todd met me there, with his parents, and I had one hell of a time signing him. Todd's father had been in the Tigers' organization, so he knew his way around baseball. God, he gave me a hassle. I made my offer but he thought Todd should get more. For three or four hours we wrangled back and forth. I stuck to my guns, though, and after a while he gave in. He just wanted the best deal for his son, and later he told me so.

"Tony," he said, "it took a lot of guts for a guy like you to come into this area and look at my boy. There's good ballplayers around here, but too many of them get caught up in gangs. That's the heart of the problem. If a kid has to join a gang he's in trouble. But if he has the opportunity to get out and make something of himself, like you've offered, then there's hope. I tried to get him the best deal I could. But I realize it's the opportunity that counts, and at least I'll know he's got the chance a lot of kids don't get."

Todd Cruz capitalized on that opportunity. Now he is an established major leaguer. But he has survived two critical tests since I signed him, and I feel his tough nature and determination have allowed him to pass both with flying colors.

The first came early in his professional career. Todd had probably the best throwing arm of any infielder I've seen. He was also very quick — he even walked quickly — and had great hands. Defense was definitely his strong suit.

But Todd never hit well. His highest average in the minors was .231 with Reading in 1976, and his ability with the bat was a concern. At spring training one year, with Dallas Green and Lee Elia, one of Todd's former coaches, looking on, there was much discussion on whether we would keep Todd or have to let him go.

But Todd took that time to be outstanding. He ran well, fielded flawlessly, threw better than ever, and even hit. He just did everything right.

I wanted to keep Todd in the organization, but we traded him to Kansas City in 1979 for Doug Bird. Todd didn't have a good year with the Royals, hitting just .203 in fifty-six games. He started 1980 with California, then was traded, ironically, to the White Sox. But it was in Chicago that Todd really started to come on. As the White Sox regular shortstop he hit .232 in ninety games and seemed to have found a home. Things were looking good when Todd's second critical test came, a back injury that sidelined him for the entire 1981 season. Many wondered if he could come back. Perhaps the White Sox didn't. They traded him to Seattle.

Todd responded with his outstanding 1982 season, though, hitting over three times as many homers and driving in almost twice as many runs as he had in his entire major league career. Todd Cruz had arrived, and he punctuated his rise to the top by helping Baltimore win the World Series.

Sometimes in this business of scouting you have to go into places you wouldn't normally go into. Sometimes it pays off; sometimes not. But when you see a player like Todd Cruz rise from the gang-infested world of the inner city to the pinnacle of major league baseball, well, it all seems worthwhile.

Two-Bagger

◆————————————————————◆

Casey Lopata and Gene Dziadura, two of Tony Lucadello's top part-time scouts, are mentioned often throughout this book. Usually they are the central figures in the signing of one player or another, but there was one instance when both Lopata and Dziadura, along with a legendary figure of Canadian baseball, indirectly collaborated on one of the rarest moments in Lucadello's career as a scout. It was a twin-kill, so to speak, the signing in one day of two future major leaguers.

Back in the early days of 1961 I received reports on two possible prospects. Casey Lopata sent me the scoop on a talented boy from Detroit named Alex Johnson. About the same time I received a note from Gene Dziadura saying there was a boy from Canada, a boy named Johnny Upham I might be interested in. I decided to check them both out for myself.

Although Johnny Upham was from Canada, he played most of his baseball in Detroit. Alex Johnson was already a well-known name there. He played on the same Northwestern High School team as Willie Horton, a powerhouse team that won the Detroit prep championship in 1961. Every scout in the league was after Horton, but Alex drew quite a crowd too.

Johnny Upham went to Assumption High School in Windsor,

Canada, where he was a student of the pioneer of Canadian baseball, Fr. Cullen. Over eighty and still going strong the last time I saw him, Fr. Cullen brought baseball to a world that had none. Few Canadian colleges offered the sport, but Fr. Cullen made sure they had it at Assumption High School. Blessed with an intense love for the game, Fr. Cullen outfitted a team year after year, though how he did it on his shoestring budget I'll never know. If I had some extra bats or balls or gloves in the trunk of my car I gave them to him, but he probably had to beg, borrow, and possibly even steal the rest of his equipment.

I scouted both players heavily and decided I would like to sign them both. And on a clear sunny day in the summer of '61 I did just that, signing Alex Johnson in the morning and Johnny Upham that night. Though signed on the same day, however, Upham would start his professional career almost a year ahead of Johnson. That was because of the rare circumstances surrounding the deal.

I signed Johnson to a contract shortly after he graduated high school and while he was playing sandlot ball. It was understood, though, that the contract would not go into effect until the following year. Signed in 1961, Alex Johnson would not actually become a professional ballplayer until 1962. That way Alex could play for any amateur team he wanted to over the summer months.

I set it up that way because of an agreement I had with a dear friend of mine, Ron Thompson. Ron coached one of the sandlot teams Alex played on and Alex, naturally, was a key man on that team. I didn't want to ruin Ron's chances for a possible championship (which, incidentally, they did win) by signing away his top player.

I know it sounds unusual, but if any man deserved to win that championship it was Ron Thompson. Ron did everything possible for the sandlot players in Detroit. One of the most dedicated men I've ever met, Ron managed teams constantly, sometimes two or three at a time. He devoted his whole life to the sandlot programs, and it showed in the tremendous pool of talent in the Detroit area. That's why Canadian players like Johnny Upham and Fergie Jenkins crossed the river to play in Detroit; the caliber of the competition was so much better there. On any given night of the week you'd see fifteen or twenty games going on and quality ballplayers all over the place. You don't see that as much anymore, though, and the overall quality of today's players has diminished with the gradual demise of sandlot ball. But that's something I'll get into later on.

Anyway, everyone agreed with the sign-now, play-later contract of mine. So I set up an appointment at the Fort Wayne Hotel in Detroit between myself, Ron Thompson, and Alex Johnson and his father. I made Alex a pretty good offer, but he didn't decide right away. A standout football player, Alex had a full scholarship to attend Michigan State if he wanted it and for a moment he thought it over. Baseball was his real love, though, and early on a July morning Alex Johnson signed the contract.

Alex had a game that night, but I told him I wouldn't be able to see him and sent Casey instead. I had taken one small gamble that day by signing Alex the day after he'd struck out four times in front of a big crowd that included a horde of scouts and farm directors. I felt I was on a roll, though, so I packed up my gear and headed across the bridge into Canada.

Where Alex Johnson was a pure outfielder, Johnny Upham was a combination player. Both he and Alex had blazing speed; they were the first two ballplayers I signed who could run the sixty-yard dash in 6.5 seconds or better. Both had outstanding arms, and Johnny had done a lot of pitching. Despite his ability as an outfielder, pitching would be Upham's ticket to the big leagues.

Signing Johnny Upham was no problem. When I got into Canada that day I met with Johnny and we dickered a while over a contract. Soon we reached a compromise, and about ten hours after I'd signed one future major leaguer, I'd signed another. It was funny when I thought about it on the drive back. While Alex Johnson was playing a game in one country, I was signing Johnny Upham to a contract in another.

Though an excellent pitcher, we recommended that Upham be converted into an outfielder and he made the transition well. His great speed, plus his good defense and natural hitting ability, were his best assets and he used them well. In his second year in the minors, Upham hit .356 with Bakersfield, California, and led the league's outfielders in fielding (.976) and assists (26). Upham made the all-star team with ease and seemed to be one of the bright, upcoming stars of the game.

The following year, though, disaster struck. Early in the season Johnny tore ligaments and ruptured the cartilage in his right knee. He had to have surgery. Knee injuries don't seem as threatening these days, what with micro-surgery and sound treatment and all. But back then there was a 50–50 chance you'd come back all right. In Johnny's case, he never did regain the speed he once had. The knee was never again as good as it once was, and his promising future as an outfielder was ended.

But Johnny still had that great arm, and once again he started pitching. He did so well that when we traded him to Chicago it was as a pitcher. He stayed with the Cubs two years (1967–68).

Alex Johnson, meanwhile, actually reached the big leagues ahead of Upham. Alex hit .303 when we brought him up to the Phillies (1964) and .294 the following season. He was traded around quite a bit after that, but when he wasn't on the trading block or injured Alex always hit well — .312 and .315 with Cincinnati (1968–69), .329 with California (1970), and .287 and .291 with Texas (1973–74).

But I always knew Alex was a hitter. When he struck out those four times the day before I signed him I knew it had been a fluke or an off-night. And to be sure, I called Casey when I returned from signing Johnny Upham and asked how Alex had done.

"You won't believe it," Casey said. "All the other scouts are heartbroken. They were all interested in signing Alex, but they found out you beat them to it this morning. Most of them wanted to see how he'd do tonight and that sold them. He had three homers and a two-bagger."

A two-bagger, huh? That word stuck with me. I guess you could say I had the same kind of day.

One Step Beyond

Picture Rod Serling on the set of a "Twilight Zone" episode and you can visualize the setting of the following tale. No last names, nor the names of any cities or towns, will be mentioned in the bulk of the story, but that is to protect the innocent as well as the guilty.

A lot of peculiar things have happened to me in my years of travel as a baseball scout. But probably the most hair-raising experience I can relate is a story I like to call, "One Step Beyond." If you remember, there was a television show by that name that featured peculiar endings that made you wonder what would have happened if, or what could have happened if, or even if it really happened at all.

I received word, in mid-August of 1953, that there was a fine young pitcher in a very small community a good distance from where I lived. He came highly recommended by a man who had caught in AAA baseball for several years, a man who had the reputation of handling some top-notch pitchers in his day. All I had to go on was that man's name, his phone number, and where he lived. I had no details on the pitcher they wanted me to check out, other than that high recommendation.

Keep in mind that I cannot mention names of people or cities involved. In fact, I signed an agreement to that effect for lawyers of the Chicago Cubs' front office. But I'll explain that later.

From my front office I learned that the pitcher would be on the mound the following Sunday, and that's where I headed. I pulled into a small town about eleven that morning, found a filling station just off the main road, and called the man (the former catcher) who was to show me this pitching prospect.

"He's not here," a woman said when I'd dialed the number.

I explained that I had to get in touch with him as soon as possible because it was very important to me. I told her who I was and why I was there — to see a boy pitch that afternoon. I knew he was to play somewhere near there, but I didn't know where and needed this man's help to guide me.

"I'm sorry to have to tell you this," she said, "but that man is my ex-husband. And right now he's in jail over in another town quite a ways from here on a very serious charge. I suggest you forget all about him and the ballplayer. Don't get involved, or you might get into more trouble than you bargained for."

Being a young, rambunctious scout who was determined to get the job done, I decided to keep going. I checked into a motel and called the jail where the man was being held.

An officer answered, and when I asked if he had a certain prisoner there by such a name, he said he did. Again I explained my situation and asked only for information concerning where and when the boy would be pitching.

The officer said he'd see what he could do, but the prisoner wouldn't cooperate. He seemed to think I was going to get him out of jail and wouldn't tell me anything until I promised to help him. Round and round we went, me saying I wasn't going to get involved and him saying I'd better if I wanted to see the young pitcher he was so high on. Finally, when he realized he wasn't going to win, he gave in. He gave me the boy's name and where he was playing. The town was about a half-hour away, and I still had plenty of time to catch the game.

Down a country road I drove until I came to a tiny burg, just a flyspeck on the map really. I stopped in front of a small store, the only one in town, as far as I could tell, and went in. The manager of the place said yes, there was a game that day, and yes, the boy I mentioned would be pitching. Then he gave me directions on how to get to the ball diamond.

Another country road led east out of town and not far out a dirt path led back to the diamond. It was a typical small-town field: skin diamond, wide-open spaces with no fence, and a backstop almost right up against home plate. A few trees marched down the third- and first-base sides.

I pulled my car off into a shallow ditch near the diamond and, because it was a real Midwest scorcher of a day, I parked under a huge, magnificent oak tree that grew near the field. I opened four doors to catch any breeze that might spring up and, since no one was there yet, I pulled out my scouting notes and waited.

Soon I heard someone coming. But when I turned around I saw that it wasn't a person: it was Mount Everest squeezed into a baseball uniform. Six-foot-five, he must have been, and easily 350 to 400 pounds.

"You the baseball scout from Chicago?" he asked, his voice rolling out like thunder down a mountainside.

"Uh, yes sir."

"Well, I'm the manager of this team," he rumbles. "My name's Bill ———— and you came down to see Chuck ———— pitch, didn't you?"

"That's right."

"Well, I got some other pretty good players on this team too," he says, and starts rattling on about how great every player on the roster is. I wasn't interested, but one look at the size of the guy and my interest seemed to grow real quickly.

The players were beginning to show up, though, and before Bill went too far with his glory feast I thanked him for his information and said I'd keep my eyes open as soon as the game started. It was a chancy ploy, but it worked. Ol' Bill jumped up and waddled off to get the game under way, using a baseball bat in either hand like a cane to support that massive body of his.

The game began a short time later, and since there was no room to sit around this dinky field I stood right up against the backstop. I wasn't more than two or three feet behind the umpire, almost right on top of the plate itself.

The first few innings went well. The pitcher had talent. Inning after inning he sat the other team down without a hit, but the competition left something to be desired. One annoyance, though, was Big Bill. After every single inning he'd waddle over and ask, "What d'ya think, huh? What d'ya think?" And every inning I'd say it was too early to tell. Then he'd waddle off again, always with a baseball bat in hand, sometimes two.

A small crowd was there when the game started, and more drifted in later on. Soon there were forty-five or fifty people standing just like me around the backstop. They were all pointing at me, saying how I was a scout from the Chicago Cubs come to look at their star pitcher; how Chuck had won sixteen ball games; how it looked like Chuck was going to make the big leagues. Things like that. Small-town talk, how rumors spread and all.

But way in the back of this group, back where I couldn't see because these people were crowded all around me, there was a smaller group. They were drinking, they were loud, and they were talking in another vein altogether. Parts of their conversation I could overhear and those parts I didn't like. They were saying how I was going to break up a great team by taking the star pitcher away and how I was going to ruin baseball in the town by stealing their hero.

That bothered me. I don't like to be around those kind of people, especially when they're drinking. And the more they drank, the meaner they got.

With that in mind, and my scouting report complete, I decided to get out while I could. I figured I'd seen enough after five innings to tell Bill in a nice way that although Chuck had talent, I didn't think he was ready to try professional ball just yet.

Bill, though, barred my escape.

"What d'ya think, huh?" he said for the fifth time.

"I'll be honest with you, Bill," I said. "I don't think Chuck is ready yet. He needs more seasoning."

Never have fewer words let so much hell loose. The words were barely out of my mouth when Bill flew into a rage. He took one of the bats he had constantly with him and started waving it over his head, screaming and hollering that I had run his ballplayer down; that even though his boy was 16-0 and throwing a no-hitter I thought he was no good; that I had insulted him and all the fans there. On and on he ranted in that deep, bellowing voice of his, like a maddened bull looking for someone to gore.

Bill's tirade didn't do the surrounding fans any good either. Stirred up now, they penned me up against the backstop, punctuating every harsh word and nasty name with a shove or a poke in the chest.

Their reaction, though, was mild compared to the group way in the back. Drunker now, and a damn sight meaner, they had come up with a whole new idea.

"Let's hang him," one shouted, and the rest took up the notion. "Henry," another yelled to a small boy nearby. "Go get that rope outta my backyard. We're not gonna let this city fella get away with this. Let's string him up to that big oak."

Back at the backstop, I was still hemmed in by the manager and the mob. Even the ballplayers had stopped playing and started to get into the act.

Above it all, though, loomed Bill, shouting and brandishing that bat over his head. I kept ducking and dodging, but he kept poking it in front of my face.

"If you had any guts," he bellowed, "Chuck would show you how good a pitcher he is. You stand in against him. I heard you've played some pro ball, so why don't you go up there and see for yourself?"

Again he stuck that bat in my face. But this time I grabbed it and he let go. The crowd still surrounded me, but at least I felt a little more confident.

"All right," I said, "I'll go to bat. And if I can't hit him, I'll sign him. I'll sign him right here on home plate."

That quieted the crowd in a hurry. You could have heard a pin drop in their midst. But farther away, I could still hear the drunks yelling for Henry to get a rope.

Bill already had his plan in motion. He got his players back on the field and I could hear him telling them how they were going to show up this fancy-pants big league scout. He stood out on the field like a great walrus, waving his arms and positioning his players like he was the greatest manager alive.

I walked onto the diamond, took off my sportcoat, and laid it on home plate. There was nowhere else to hang it, and I sure didn't trust it with the crowd. Two deep holes were in the batter's box, dug by the constant scratching of spikes. But I avoided them as best I could and tried to settle into a good stance.

I saw Bill whispering to his pitcher, and I knew from my baseball experience that he was going to do one of two things — throw at me or curve me. That's all I was going to see, so I was looking for those two pitches.

I also knew, from not having had a bat in my hands since

Charlie Root and I hit a little practice in spring training, that the only thing I could hit would be something around my eyes. If the pitch was out and away or low, I knew I'd have a hard time following it. My timing was off, but if he threw it up around my eyes and it hung there, I figured I could stay with it, get the bat on it, and maybe pull it. The kid wasn't a professional and he wasn't throwing that hard. And if he did get it up it was going to hang, because he didn't have that good of a curve ball anyway.

I had to figure him out. I had to make an impression. I had to hit him. There seemed no other way.

I tried one last time to reason with Bill as he walked off the field. "Look what you're doing," I said. "Look what you've created. A ballgame's been disrupted, these fans back here are mad as hell, and that group over there wants to string me up."

"They ought to hang you," he spat and walked away.

So that was that. I stood on a stage in a play I didn't want to perform in. But I had been forced into the role, and there was only one way to act it out.

Trying to relax, I stepped into the box. Tension hung over the field like a fog. The pitcher went into his windup, delivered, and — Good Lord! — it was a curve. The very first pitch he threw was a curve and it was perfect — for me, that is. Lazily it hung there like a big fat watermelon and I hit it dead center. I wasn't going to try and lift, since it was up a bit high. So I tried to hit down a little and the ball sailed into left field on a semi-line drive. The leftfielder probably could have caught it, but Bill in his infinite wisdom had moved him in, thinking a little guy like me couldn't have any power. Over his head the ball floated and, with no fence, just kept rolling.

Only a second I watched the ball; there were more important things at hand.

When I hit the ball everyone just stopped. Their silence hung in the air as they stood frozen. Taking the lull as a chance to get away, I threw away the bat, grabbed my coat, and headed for my car.

In my haste to get rid of the bat, though, I tossed it behind me without looking. Purely by accident, it hit Bill right in the leg.

Bill's roar shook the cobwebs from the crowd and again they came at me. Only Bill himself saved me from being swarmed over.

"Don't anybody touch him, but don't let him get away," he

yelled, throwing up his arms and telling the crowd to form a circle. "I'm gonna take care of him myself."

Trapped now, Bill and I began a strange dance. Again and again he lunged at me, but I avoided him with ease. I used my coat like a matador's cape to feint him out of position, and his vast weight made him clumsy and slow.

But the crowd, seeing that the ring was too big to be of much help to Bill, began to close in. Closer and closer it came until there was no way I could avoid another bull-like charge from the big manager. Then, just when Bill was tensing for one final lunge, a whirlwind hit me from behind and sent me sprawling. It knocked the wind out of me and jarred my senses, but I realized the drunks — about ten of them — had hit the circle like a tornado. They had gotten a rope from somewhere (either Henry had submitted to the threats or one of the drunks had gotten it himself) and had formed their long-sought lynch party. A noose was slipped over my head and I was soon being dragged toward the big oak.

This story might have ended right there if it hadn't been for the condition of the mob. In their drunken state they couldn't get the other end of the rope over the branch. They got lucky on about the tenth throw, though, and several willing hands got ready to hoist me up.

I don't know if they were really going to go through with it or not, but just when I'd prepared myself to meet my maker, I heard sirens off in the distance. Sweet, sweet music it was, and growing louder by the second.

The men that were holding me up suddenly let go and I fell, stunned, right on my back. I lay there a minute or two and when I looked up the crowd had scattered. They were gone, every one of them.

I was getting back to my feet when two policemen came up.

"What the hell's going on here?" they asked.

"Nothing. Nothing."

"Nothing? Then what's this here rope doing around your neck? They try to hang you or something?"

"No, no," I said. "Please. Just let me get in my car and follow you to the highway."

They questioned me for quite a while, but I wouldn't tell them anything. Finally, they gave up. I followed them to the main road and headed out of there.

Later, I found out that the owner of the store I had stopped at had been at the game. When he saw what was brewing, he went for the cops.

I probably owe him my life, but then again I don't know. That's why I call the story "One Step Beyond." When people ask me if they really would have gone through with it — if they really would have hanged me — I can only answer, "I don't know. I really don't."

The reason I cannot mention specific names or towns came about in this way:

Quite some time after this had happened, Ray Hayworth and I were in Utica, New York, representing the Chicago Cubs at an all-sports clinic. A sports announcer there wanted to interview me, but he said all the baseball scouts he had interviewed always said the same things: what they looked for in a ballplayer, who they had signed, the best area to scout. These were things fans had heard a thousand times. He wanted to know if I could relate a story of something that happened to me while scouting. I told him I had a good story, but that I wouldn't mention any names or places. I still wasn't too sure about this whole thing yet. So we worked out the details and I told my story on the radio.

A few days later, his station started getting swamped with mail. People wanted to know if they really did hang me, who I was, where they buried me, what happened to the people who did this cruel thing. You'd be surprised the impressions people get when they hear something like that on the radio. It was like "War of the Worlds" all over again.

The radio station didn't know what to do with all the mail, so they sent it to Wrigley Field. And when Jim Gallagher, our general manager, and Jack Sheehan, our farm director, and the rest of the front office read this mail, they decided to call Mr. P. K. Wrigley himself. After he had read some of the mail, he called me into his office.

"These letters pertaining to a story about a hanging, are they true?" he asked.

"They're true," I said. "It happened last August."

"Well, then, this is what I want you to do," he said. "Go to a radio station, make a recording of that story in your words, and bring it to me."

I did as he asked, and he listened to the whole story in full.

After a consultation with his lawyers, P. K. Wrigley asked me to see him again. This time, though, the meeting was to be at the Wrigley Building, their main office downtown. I knew it must be important.

There were about ten lawyers there when I arrived. All had listened to the recording.

They stressed how fortunate it was that I had not mentioned any names on my first radio broadcast. That was a key point. Then they had me sign forms stating that I would never mention the names of anyone involved in the story or the place where it happened.

The incident, they felt, could have shed a bad light on baseball. And to protect the integrity of the sport, I signed the papers.

To this day I have never broken that contract. And I never will.

Debt of a Salesman

◆──────────────────────────────◆

Baseball scouts must be the world's greatest salesmen, because they deal in that rare commodity called people. They not only have to sell themselves and their ball club to the prospect, they also have to sell the prospect to their front office.

Tony Lucadello, like most good scouts, was a good salesman. But it took a trip to Jamesville, Wisconsin, and nearly a year of hard work to determine how dedicated a salesman he could be.

Back in the early '50s, when I was still scouting for the Cubs, I covered the Midwest from Ohio to Wisconsin and from Canada to Kentucky. All through this area I ran tryout camps, a quality-from-quantity system where we'd bring in a couple hundred young ballplayers and hope to find a few with major league potential.

It was at one of these tryout camps in Jamesville, Wisconsin, that a fifteen-year-old outfielder named Bobby Haney caught my eye. Haney was a fine-looking athlete, and despite his age the boy greatly impressed me and my staff. I was certain we had a real prospect on our hands.

Now my job became one of patience and PR (prospect relations). I had to keep in close contact with the boy. I had to meet his parents, wine 'em and dine 'em, and almost become a part of the family. It would be another three years before Bobby could sign a professional contract, and by then much could depend on a scout's closeness to a prospect and his family. Back then, when every young ballplayer was virtually a free agent, that sort of thing meant a lot — more so, it seems, than today.

So for three years, Jamesville was a familiar stop on my route through the upper Midwest. Whenever I was in the area I made it a point to see Bobby Haney and visit with his family.

But Bobby Haney wasn't the type of athlete you could cover up and keep under wraps. By the time he graduated from high school, almost every major league team knew about him. And a bunch of teams wanted to sign him.

My visits to Jamesville, though, and the closeness that grew between the Haneys and me, had merit. As the time drew near for Bobby to sign, his parents came to me and said I had the choice of talking to Bobby anytime I wanted. They said I could be the first scout to see Bobby, or the second, or the third. It was entirely up to me.

I told them I wanted to be last. That way I would have some indication what his best offer was, and I could see if I could match it or not.

So one by one the scouts trickled in and out of the Haney house. Some spent quite a bit of time there; others were gone before I knew it.

After the sixth had left, the Haneys called and said it was my turn. I asked Bobby's father if he wanted to tell me his best offer, or if he preferred to just let me lay my cards on the table. He favored the latter so I made my pitch. It wasn't too high, mind you, but it was what we considered a reasonable proposition.

"My gosh, Tony," Bobby's father said, a terrible disappointment showing in his face, "every club in here made a better offer than you just did."

"They did?"

"They did! All six of them."

Well, then, I didn't know what to do. In those days I wasn't authorized to give extra money to prospects. The club was very tight and close with us scouts. They had quoted me a certain amount and that was all I could give.

"I'm sorry," I told him. "That's the best offer I can make. I can't come up with a better deal than that."

"We're very disappointed," he said. "We wanted our boy to sign with you. You've been good to us the last three years. We know you've helped Bobby, and done a lot for him."

"Yes, you can't evaluate that in terms of money," I said. "Those are things you just can't buy."

"Well, Tony, I'm sorry then too. But I'm afraid we'll have to turn you down."

That ended the bargaining, for all intents and purposes. But we sat and talked for a while, as good friends often do. Just because I didn't sign their son didn't mean the closeness born in those three years we'd known each other was nothing.

Finally, though, it was time to leave. I knew it was useless to press the issue, so I decided to be on my way. I wished Bobby good luck, wherever he might wind up, and headed for my car.

Bobby's father had followed me out, and just as we neared my car he suddenly asked, "Do you know what type of business I'm in Tony?"

I assured him I didn't.

"Well, come on around the house. I'll show you."

Behind the Haney house was a cinder-block building, bigger than your standard garage, but not a huge structure. And on the front of this building, in big, bold letters, was a sign reading: HANEY'S PANCAKE MIX. He took me inside the building, where three women were running machinery that made this pancake mix, boxed it, and put the boxes into cartons.

"You make Haney's Pancake Mix?" I asked. "I never heard of it."

"Of course you haven't," he said. "It's only sold around here. I got the recipe when I was in the service and started my own little factory back here. I do most of my business with restaurants, since they buy in bulk. Those smaller boxes are for grocery stores, but there's my problem. I'm pretty well known in southern Wisconsin and northern Illinois, but it's hard for me to get a foothold any-where else. As I tried to expand I kept running up against the na-tional brand names. Theirs may be a little cheaper than mine, but I feel mine's a better product."

"Well, I don't know," I said. "Pancakes are a little out of my line."

"But you know baseball, Tony. And I'll tell you what. You want to sign Bobby, right?"

"Sure."

"But you want to sign him for only what you can give him, right?"

"Yes, only the offer I made before."

"All right, then. If you really want to sign Bobby you're going to have to make a deal."

"What kind of deal?" I asked.

"You're going to have to sell 100 cases of Haney's Pancake Mix, but only in Ohio. I want Haney's Pancake Mix to be known throughout the state. My name and address are on every box. If you can get it spread around Ohio, maybe you can help my little business branch out and grow."

It didn't take much thought to sway my decision. I was a young scout, full of energy, and I thought I could conquer anything.

"You got yourself a deal."

He made me sign a contract, then an agreement saying that if I didn't sell all 100 cases, I'd have to buy the rest myself. Then we threw ten cases in the trunk of my car (maybe I could sell them on the way back to Ohio or something) and made plans for him to ship me the rest.

Then it was my turn with the contract, and Bobby Haney finally put his name on the dotted line. He never did make it to the major leagues, though. That's unfortunate, because he was a fine athlete. And looking back it seems all the work I went through to sign him may have been nothing but smoke. But scouts had to do things like that. It might have paid off. That was the chance I took.

Trouble was, just when I thought I had the hardest part over with, it was actually just beginning.

It was a week to ten days before I got back into Fostoria. The first thing I did was to call my wife and tell her I was home. Somehow, though, I don't think she was all that pleased to hear my voice.

"Tony Lucadello, what have you gotten into now? We've got cases and cases of pancake mix all over this house. The hallways are blocked, the bedrooms are full, and the closets are jammed right up to the Christmas decorations. What have you gotten mixed up in?"

"Pancakes," I said. "But it's a long story, Virginia. I'll tell you when I get home."

Even after the story unfolded, though, Virginia's mind was closed to the whole idea.

"You can't sell that stuff," she said. "I've never heard of it and no one else around here has either. People are going to buy the product they've bought all along and, besides, this one's even more expensive."

"Don't get excited," I soothed. "I'm going to sell it. I'm a great salesman. You just watch. I'll take a couple cases down to Hammer's, and a couple more over to Stark's. We've dealt with them for years. They'll take four or five cases off our hands real quick."

Off I went, my enthusiasm casting out all doubt. I figured I'd hit Stark's first, a little community store near our house, then waltz on over to Hammer's, down the block.

"Sure, I'll take two cases," Mr. Stark said. "But I can't put them in the store. I'll take them home with me."

I knew he was buying them just because I was a regular customer, and that's not the way I wanted it to be.

"Don't patronize me," I said. "This pancake mix has to be set up in the store, just like the brand names. Take the Aunt Jemima and Pillsbury off the shelf if you have to, but at least put it out so people can see it."

"Sorry," he said. "Can't do it. I have to stick with the things that sell or I'm out of business. I can't just take a chance on something I've never seen or heard about before."

"Well, you don't want these two cases then," I said, picking up my load and heading for the door.

Beaten once, I took only half as much enthusiasm into Hammer's and walked out with none. It was the same story there. No room and no interest in a no-name product.

Dejected, I headed home. Virginia got a good laugh when she saw me, but we both shared the same problem — what to do with 100 cases of pancake mix. You could stack it into furniture, but it was too hard to sit on for long. You could wrap it as presents and give it away, but you could lose friends and alienate relatives that way. And, Lord knows, I didn't want pancakes morning, noon, and night for the rest of my life.

Slowly, though, an idea emerged, a perfect angle for our dilemma.

"Virginia," I said, "I want you to get on the phone and call ten or fifteen of your friends. Tell them you want them to make two calls for you, one to Stark's and another to Hammer's.

"Tell them to ask for Haney's Pancake Mix. Now, the store will say that they don't have it and that they've never heard of it. But tell your friends to say they thought they carried it, and if they don't have it, well, that's all they wanted."

So Virginia got on the phone, called her friends, and started my plan going. I waited about an hour, hour-and-a-half, then headed right for Stark's. But Mr. Stark saw me coming, and before I was halfway across the street, he was hollering at me.

"Hey, Tony," he shouted. "What was that you were in here trying to sell a couple of hours ago?"

"Oh, just Haney's Pancake Mix. Why?"

"Holy smokes," he says. "I must have had fifteen or twenty calls for that just today."

"The stores north of town must carry it," I said, "but they must have run out. Everyone probably thought you carried it too."

"Well, I'll buy those two cases off of you now," he said. "And I might need an extra case or two to be safe."

Then I headed for Hammer's, and for the second time that day the story was the same. Only this time I came out of there smiling.

I worked that angle all winter all over the state of Ohio. I'd walk into a store, get turned down, then have friends call and ask for Haney's Pancake Mix. When I went back to the store, they almost always bought a few cases.

It took a lot of months, a lot of miles, and a lot of stores, but finally I got all 100 cases sold. I figured that paid the debt and wiped the slate clean, but my little stint as a pancake mix salesman came back to haunt me some years ago.

I was at a father-and-son banquet in Lancaster, Ohio, and decided to tell this story. But right in the middle of it, some guy jumped up and yelled, "Tony, you son-of-a-gun. I'm one of the guys who bought two cases of Haney's Pancake Mix from you, and you know what? They're still in my store. I still got them. I never could sell a box of that stuff."

Treetop Scout

The cloak-and-dagger, behind-the-scenes method of scouting that Tony Lucadello employed in his pursuit of Mike Schmidt earned him more than a few good ballplayers: it earned him a reputation.

Unseen and unheard, Lucadello slipped like a phantom through ball-parks across the Midwest. Other scouts who had not seen him all season would be baffled at how Lucadello could sign a player away from them, not realizing that Tony had probably seen the prospect as often as, if not more than, they did.

If you don't believe it, just ask Denny Galehouse, a former major leaguer himself and later a scout with Detroit, St. Louis, the New York Mets, and most recently San Diego.

This goes back quite a few years when I was scouting for the Phils. I had been keeping tabs on a Columbus boy, a pitcher/outfielder from West High School named John Glenn Morlan. He was a fine prospect, specifically as a pitcher, and definitely no secret. A lot of clubs were hoping to get him.

Morlan played for Dave Koblentz at West High School, a man I had dealt with before. Another friend of mine, Fred Mocra, coached at Whetstone High, and when I learned the two teams were playing early one spring I decided I'd better go down and see what they had. The Morlan boy was the one I really wanted to see, but I was going to keep my eyes open for any talent I could find. The June draft wasn't that far off and I, along with most of the other scouts across the country, had our reports to get in.

A delay here and a stopover there cost me time, though, and I pulled into Columbus behind schedule. I knew I'd have to hurry to catch the West-Whetstone game so I quickly checked into a motel, threw everything in the room, and raced to the game. I noticed it was overcast as I left the motel and realized I'd left my raincoat behind. But I was late and I wasn't going to waste time going back to get it.

The game was already under way when I reached the Whetstone field, but I hadn't missed much. It had also started to rain, not enough to stop the game but a steady drizzle just the same.

A line of trees stretched down the third base line of the ball diamond, and it was under one of them that I took shelter. I had a good view of the field and noticed right off that Morlan wasn't pitching; he was playing in the outfield. That was all right. At least I'd still get a good look at the boy.

I also noticed that, behind home plate, there were six or eight scouts up in the stands with their raincoats up over their heads to keep their clipboards dry. Denny Galehouse was there, Fred Shaffer of the White Sox, "Mo" Mozelli of the Cards, and a bunch of others. That wasn't so good. I like to keep my scouting private, and the last thing I wanted was other scouts knowing who I was after.

I was debating between whether to take off or find a good hiding place when I looked up into the tree and saw a crook about fifteen feet up. I'd still be able to see the field, I figured, and the leaves overhead would keep me dry. So I scrambled my old bones up that tree and settled myself down.

Morlan, who pitched for the Pirates for a couple of years, never did take the mound that game. But I got a good look at him anyway. I had a perfect view of the field from that fork in the tree and stayed dry besides. The damp must have gotten to the other scouts, however, or maybe they'd just seen enough, because in the sixth inning they all got up to leave. En masse they strolled out the gate and down the third base line toward the parking lot. Sure enough, they stopped right under my tree and shook some of the rain off their coats before they made a dash for their cars.

"You know," one of them said to the others, "I haven't seen that Lucadello all spring. Where the hell's he been?"

"Aw, you know how he is," Galehouse said. "He never shows himself if he sees other scouts around. I'll bet he's hiding somewhere."

"It wouldn't surprise me if he's over by the first base line," one of the scouts said.

"Naw, he's probably behind the outfield fence, over by the schoolyard," said another.

"Forget it," Galehouse said. "You'd as soon find Lucadello over there as you would up this here tree." And laughing and chuckling to themselves the scouts headed for their cars.

I damn near busted a gut. I was laughing so hard through the whole thing I thought I'd fall and break my neck. Tears came to my eyes and my side ached, but I kept quiet until they'd gone. Then I climbed down, got into my car, and left.

That could have been the end of it had it not been for a little instance a few months later. It was early September and I was scouting the Stan Musial World Series in Battle Creek, Michigan. The tournament was a big thing. Because a lot of baseball scouts always showed up, a special section behind home plate had been set up for them at Post Park.

Day late and a dollar short, I was again late. I showed up after all the other scouts were there and didn't have time to get a pass. I paid my own way in and sat in the bleachers, but that was fine by me. It gave me more freedom to move around and roam where I wanted.

Since the first batter was a righthander I positioned myself down the first base line. That way I could see the frontal planes of his body, his hands and feet, and most importantly his eyes. But the other scouts saw me, too, and I noticed a pretty good discussion going on between them. It wasn't too long before a couple of the guys came over.

"Tony," one said. "We got an argument going on and Galehouse is even betting money. He says this is the first time you've seen him all year."

"You go back and tell Denny," I said, "that I've seen him seven times before today."

Off they went, but in a little while a whole group of scouts came trooping over. Galehouse led the way and he stopped below us, looking up at me and the fans in the stands.

"Lucadello," he said. "Name one time you saw me at a ball-game before today."

"That's easy," I yelled down to him. "Remember last spring when you and a bunch of these other guys were looking at the Morlan boy from Columbus West? Remember how it rained and you stopped under that tree to stay dry? And remember how you said you wouldn't be surprised if I was up in that tree hiding from you guys? You shoulda looked up in that tree, Denny, 'cause I was up there."

I don't know if Denny appreciated that (or if he lost much on his bets), but the scouts and the fans got a charge out of it. You know, I had a pretty good time at that tournament.

A Cab Ride
Through Hell

◆────────────────◆

Wherever there was a speck of baseball talent, Tony Lucadello went look-ing for it. From the backwoods of Canada and the boondocks of rural Indiana and Kentucky to the sandlots of Detroit and ghettos of Chicago, Lucadello went prospecting. It is because of that gutsy determination that he signed so many major league ballplayers.

It wasn't always easy, not by a long shot. Lucadello ventured into some real hell-holes of the Midwest and, as he related in "One Step Beyond," it was often dangerous.

Like that earlier story, the signing of Fred Andrews has a vein of fear running through it. The circumstances were similar to Lucadello's signing of Todd Cruz — only the scenery was different.

Inner-city Chicago in the early '70s was an ugly sort of arena. Gang lords played Caesar with the citizens; cold city streets, littered with the decay of the ghetto and lined with the rat-trap tenements of the poor, were the Coliseum.

For Freddy Andrews, it was home.

I heard about Freddy Andrews while visiting my sister in Chi-cago. I was told that the boy was exceptionally quick, though small, and was quite well known around the sandlots of the city.

I tried to look the boy up, but came up with nothing but dead-ends and empty leads. It was as if he had vanished into thin air. A month or two later, however, I got word that Fred Andrews had been sent to Cincinnati. It's my understanding, from the information I gathered, that one of the gangs in Fred's neighborhood wanted to recruit him, and that he'd been threatened with all sorts of crap if he didn't join them. Fred's mother (his parents were separated) wanted to keep Fred away from that type of lifestyle, so she sent him to stay with relatives in Cincinnati. A friend of the family (I think he had coached Fred earlier) went along.

Fred enrolled at Lincoln Heights High School, and that's where he made his mark. Fred drew a lot of attention, especially his senior year when he led his team to the Ohio Class A state championship. For a while, though, it looked as if his team wouldn't even make it through the tournament. The school was going to be consolidated and didn't want to pump money into a baseball program that wasn't going to be around the next year. But some help came through (hell, I even donated some bats and balls to the team) and they went all the way. Freddy had a great tournament, especially in the championship when he made two diving catches and scored the winning run.

On my recommendation, we drafted Fred in the eighth round of the 1970 draft. But the draft had been held before the state tournament was over, and you can't sign a player until he's done with high school commitments. By the time I got back in contact with Fred, after I'd signed a few other players we'd drafted, the finals were over and he'd gone back to Chicago.

I had to get Fred's name on the contract, so I told him I'd fly to Chicago. I told him what hotel I'd be at (the same one our club stayed at when the Phillies were in town) and that I'd call him when I got in to set up an appointment where we could negotiate and handle the actual signing.

I knew the kind of neighborhood Fred lived in, so I hoped to handle everything right from my hotel. But when I checked in and phoned Fred again, I quickly found out I had to make other plans. Two rival gangs, it seems, were raising hell with the area and it wasn't safe for anyone to get in or out of the neighborhood. Could I, Fred asked, meet him at his place?

I didn't relish the idea of walking into a gang war, but what else could I do? I had to get Freddy's signature on the contract and time was running out. I set up a meeting at seven. That way his mother, who worked at a hospital until six, would have plenty of time to slip home herself and be on hand for the negotiations.

Knowing what kind of neighborhood I was going into, I prepared myself accordingly. I didn't bring my briefcase, or carry anything in my hands. I took off my watch and rings, pulled a few bills from my wallet, and left. I wished I'd had some older, grubbier clothes, but my sportcoat would have to do. I didn't even wear my hat, and I'm never seen without my hat.

I went out the front of the hotel, but I didn't jump into the first taxi that pulled up. Instead I waited until one driven by a black guy came along, then I got in.

"4848 South State Street," I told him.

He just sat there.

"I said 4848 South State Street."

But he still didn't budge.

"What's the matter?" I asked. "You deaf?"

"Nope," he said. "But you seem to be plenty stupid. You know what that neighborhood's like? I'm black and I don't even go near that area. You just better reconsider 'cause you don't want to be seen down there."

"I gotta get there," I said. "I got a business engagement."

"Sorry," he said, "I ain't taking you."

"If you don't, somebody else will," I said. "I'll just sit here and wait for another cab. I'll get there one way or another."

Maybe the Lucadello luck was with me, or maybe the guy realized that someone else could screw me over good. Whatever, he decided to drive me to Freddy's apartment, and I'll always respect that man for his courage and honesty.

"I'll take you," he said, "but on my terms. There's a few rules we got to lay down. First, the fare's gonna be about four dollars, so pay me now."

I gave him a five and told him to keep the change.

"Now," he said. "When I get to a certain street I'm gonna tell you to get on the floor and you better do it. If anybody sees you in here it could get hairy real quick. I don't remember the last time a cab's been in that area and come back out again, so I'm gonna work fast. You won't have much time, so I'm gonna drive like hell and slam on the brakes where you want to be. It'll be a gray apartment house on your right. You jump out and run — run as fast as you can for that front door. If anyone sees you . . . if they catch you . . . I can't stop and help you."

"Fine," I said, but I could already feel my heart pounding a quick rhythm against my rib cage.

On cue, a short time later, the cabbie told me to get down. It occurred to me, lying there on the floor, that he could easily drive anywhere, tell me to get out and run, and I'd jump, not knowing if I was in front of Fred's apartment house or some gang leader's lair. It wasn't a comforting thought.

Through the dark streets of inner Chicago we sped. Judging by the passing street lights, we were doing a pretty good clip.

There was no warning to destination's end. Just a lurch, the screech of brakes, and a hoarse, "Go."

I shot out the door, not even bothering to close it, and ran. In front of me was the apartment house, just as the cabbie had described it, with a paint-peeled front door. It opened a crack as I bounded up the steps, but my fears melted away when I saw Fred Andrews inside. He'd sensed I might need some looking after, and had come down to meet me. Grabbing me by the arm, he pulled me inside.

Just before the door closed I glanced up the street. A solitary vehicle, a yellow cab, went racing by, ran a red light, and disappeared into the night.

Freddy and I went upstairs to his apartment. His mother was there. We discussed the contract. Terms were agreed upon and he signed. It went smooth as silk.

We talked — Fred, his mother, and I — for a while. His mother wanted to know if, with his signing bonus, we could help them find a better place to live. Our organization had some connections with real estate agencies in the Chicago area and, eventually, we were able to find them a better neighborhood. We chatted on, forgetting for a time what was just outside the door, just down the street.

I felt safe and secure sitting there in the Andrews home, but it couldn't last. I'd gotten in. Now how the hell would I get back out? I asked if I could call a cab, but Fred said they wouldn't come to that section of town. He couldn't believe I'd gotten one to come there in the first place.

Fred had a plan, though. It would cost me some money, but he had a friend who would get me out of the neighborhood for a price. He had a car waiting in the alley, and for $20 he'd slip me out.

So Fred took me to the basement of the building. He found an old canvas cloth and wrapped it around me. Then we crept out a back door and stepped into the alley.

His friend was there and again I was hustled onto the floor of a car. Again I had the same doubts as before. The darkness under the canvas fostered nightmares of where I was going and what destination lay ahead.

The driver finally said I could sit up, though, and I was surprised to see how far we'd gone. My hotel was just ahead. I got out at the entrance, paid the man, and walked inside. Off in the distance, the screaming wail of a siren split the night.

Fred Andrews didn't play much for the Phillies. He was only with the big club twice — 1976 and 1977 — before we traded him. Freddy's a winner, though. He proved that when he was named to all-star teams in the Instructional League and Eastern League with Reading, where he led the league in at bats (506) and hit .273 and stole 58 bases. Freddy's come up the hard way, but he made it.

Fred Andrews is also a living example of the way baseball can affect a young man's life. He could have been swallowed up in the gang system that ruled his neighborhood. In the ghettos, young men with no jobs and nothing to do have no outlet for their natural enthusiasm, so they form gangs. It's a destructive system.

Fred Andrews proved there's another alternative. He made it. So can others.

The Impatient
Slugger

◆————————————◆

Not all of the ballplayers Tony Lucadello scouted ended up in the big leagues. There was a big difference, naturally, in the number he saw and the number he signed.

Some just couldn't make the grade. Others lacked dedication or desire. A few were just downright unlucky.

And then there was Johnson, a prodigious hitter who seemed blessed with all the tools. Johnson's only problem, though, was that he hit one home run too many. Sound strange? Not when you know all the details.

It all started . . .

. . . one season in spring training. As I did every year with the Cubs I was down in Florida, where we had various camps. Back then we didn't have complexes where you'd bring in everyone in your system. We had camps; two or three in Florida, another in Georgia, another in Illinois, one in Missouri.

That particular year I was working with the group in Haines City, Florida. We had four clubs training there, but only two diamonds. So one morning when I wasn't doing much, Jack Sheehan, our farm director, cornered me.

"Tony," he said, "I've got an assignment for you. We have a chance to buy a ballplayer on a conditional basis and I want you to

102

check him out. Before we put any money down, we have thirty days to watch him play. So you follow him around, keep an eye on him, and let us know when you've made up your mind."

The boy's name was Johnson — Ralph or Ron or Roger or something. I forget, so I'll just call him Johnson. He was the property of the St. Louis Cardinals.

The Cards were also training in Florida, so I found out which camp he was at and motored on down there. With about a week left in spring training, I wanted to get a quick start.

I liked what I saw when I got my first glimpse of Johnson. He was a big, strong boy with a good and accurate arm. He had below average speed for an outfielder and his defense needed some work, but there was potential there.

What amazed me about Johnson, though, was his bat. Where other hitters punched the ball, he punished it. Where others lifted the ball out of the park, he launched it.

Johnson was, without a doubt, one of the most powerful sluggers I'd ever seen. Day after day in that final week of spring training, I sat in awe as he smashed tape-measure home runs well over the outfield wall.

By the end of the week I had a glowing report on the young slugger. And when I learned he'd been assigned to the Huntington Redbirds, a Class C team in West Virginia, I followed.

Johnson's debut in Huntington was a repeat of spring training. There wasn't a ballpark, it seemed, capable of containing the rockets that flew from his bat. He belted five homers the first week alone, a few of them tape-measure jobs, and my report on him got better and better.

Huntington went on the road then, and again I followed. In their first game the Redbirds faced a crafty veteran of the minor leagues, a gray wolf whose fastball wasn't good enough for the majors but whose curve ball was good enough for the minors.

Four times Johnson stepped in against those slow, tantalizing curves. Four times he waved that big bat at a third strike and headed back to the dugout.

"It was just a bad day," his manager told him. "You'll snap out of it."

But that veteran pitcher must have passed the word along to his teammates. The next day Johnson again saw nothing but breaking stuff, and again he went hitless. The fences once more were safe; the hammer had been broken.

Word spread like wildfire through the league: "Johnson can't hit the breaking ball." And every junk-baller in the league took it to heart. Johnson saw every curve, changeup, slider, and knuckler in the book, and probably a spitter or two. For almost two weeks that man never saw a fastball. They even threw him breaking stuff on a 3-0 count.

Usually, Johnson would strike out. But even when he did get his bat on the ball it would only be a dribbler to the infield or easy pop fly. Never in that time did he hit the ball with the awesome power I'd seen earlier.

I had long since become leery of this young Goliath. I could see the boy had trouble with the offspeed pitching and his hitting could no longer offset his speed and defense. It was just about time to file my report, but I wanted to see him play once more to be sure.

The last time I saw Johnson was after a Friday night double-header. They played two seven-inning games. It was called twilight ball.

Johnson, naturally, saw all curve balls and didn't do anything in the first game. But his team came to life in the second. The Red-birds trailed by a run in the last of the seventh but had two men on with two outs and a pretty good hitter at the plate.

Johnson was in the on-deck circle, obviously thinking about his two-week slump. As every pitch approached the plate, he'd take an imaginary swing at it, trying to measure the speed and angle of the ball.

But the hitter in front of him rapped a drive into the gap, and it looked as though Johnson wouldn't get his last at bat. The runner on second scored easily to tie the game and, as the rightfielder wheeled and fired to the cutoff man, the second runner rounded third. For a moment it appeared there would be a play at the plate, but the relay throw came in way off line. It would be off the plate by a good fifteen to twenty feet.

The throw, however, was on a beeline for the on-deck circle — and Johnson. Maybe it was anger that prompted Johnson's next move, or the frustration of his slump. Whatever the motivation, Johnson suddenly lashed out at the baseball and knocked it out of the park.

The umpire, of course, ruled interference. The batter was called out, and the runs were disallowed.

I found Johnson a short time later, sitting on a stool in the corner of the locker room, tears streaming down his face.

"Why, Johnson, why?" the manager was screaming at him. "Why did you do it?"

"I can't really tell you, Skipper," Johnson said, wiping a huge paw across his eyes. "All I know is that for two weeks I've gone to the plate and seen curve ball after curve ball. All of a sudden I saw this fastball coming at me, beautiful and straight and just hanging there. What else could I do? I just had to swing at it."

Then Johnson, the big lug who hit one home run too many, put his head in his hands and wept.

I crumpled up my report and left it lying there on the floor.

Down on the Farm

◆————————————————————————————◆

When my ex-farm director Gene Martin went into semi-retirement, he always took a few weeks off in the summer to come down for a visit. He would check over my ballplayers, BS about the farm system, and rehash some of his own colorful baseball background. He enjoyed it, and I enjoyed having him with me.

We were staying in Richmond, Indiana, at the time and my office had informed me of a boy in Hicksville, Ohio (about sixty or seventy miles away) who was supposed to be pretty good. I had never seen him, but since my boss was down (I called him my boss because I used to work for him) I thought it was the perfect opportunity for him to see some of my talent. Gene jumped at the chance.

I called the coach of the player I wanted to see and he said the boy was pitching the next day. Perfect. Gene and I hopped into my car and off we went. About halfway there, though, it started to sprinkle. And by the time we hit Hicksville, the rain was just pouring down. The game was canceled, naturally, so we drove back.

The next day I call the coach again, and he says the game's been rescheduled for that night. Fine. Again we hop into my car and again we head for Hicksville. This time we're almost there when the rains come, and the game is canceled again. Washed out two days straight.

I was trying to find out when the game would be played when Gene started talking about catching a plane. He lived in Florida and figured it about time to head home.

"Stay just another day," I begged him, "because we're going to see that kid tomorrow whether it rains or not. I've got it all figured out."

"Okay. One more day," Gene said. "But that's it. If I don't see him tomorrow, I'm heading home."

I knew the team was supposed to play the next day, but I made some extra plans just to be safe. I called the coach and told him that if it rained and the game was canceled again, he could send the rest of his players home — but keep that pitcher and his catcher there. I told him to put them in his car and park right behind the backstop so I would know right where they were. "I'll be there," I told him. "We're going to see that boy rain or shine."

Thankfully, the coach went along with me. He knew how hard I'd been trying to see the boy and how anxious I was to show him to my boss.

With everything all set, we headed a third time toward Hicksville. We weren't even there yet when again it started to rain. By the time we pulled up to the ballpark it was pouring. But the coach was sitting there in his car, just as he said he would, and with him were the pitcher and the team's catcher. "Follow me," I yelled to him, and even though he didn't know what I was up to he followed.

We headed out of town on some country back road, but it wasn't until about three miles later that I found just the place I'd been looking for. Down a long lane stood a farm house, and beyond that two small barns. Back then, farms usually had two or three small barns instead of the one big building you see today. They'd keep feed and animals in one, machinery in the other.

"Could we use your two barns?" I asked the farmer who came to the door.

"What the hell for?"

I explained the whole situation to him, how I had a young pitcher I wanted to see throw; how the rain had washed out three games; how my boss was anxious to get home to Florida; and how he had the ideal situation for me to work the boy out. Either he knew the boy, had seen him pitch, or had heard about him, because the farmer said he'd be glad to help.

A little while later he was out there in his big, yellow slicker, sliding back the doors of his barns. We pulled up as close as we could (it was still raining cats and dogs) and jumped into one of the buildings.

Then I explained the situation to the others. They had been in the dark all this time. I kept the catcher in our barn, sent the pitcher to the other, and lined them up about sixty feet apart.

Gene, who had grown as gloomy as the weather, still wasn't sold on my plan. "Lucadello," he said, "just what the hell are you trying to prove?"

"I told you I was going to show you this pitcher," I said. "I haven't seen him yet myself, but this seemed like the only way. Just quit your growling. I'm beginning to think you're mad just because you're not on that plane to sunny Florida."

Gene didn't think it was funny. And he still wasn't all too sure of what I was up to. While the boy was warming up, Gene just stood back and watched, checking his speed, his arm movement and delivery, but not showing an inch that he cared one way or the other.

Since the boy was throwing through the rain, every so often I'd take some old rags and wipe the ball off for him. When he was good and loose, though, I walked over to him and handed him a brand new ball.

"Now son," I told him, "I want you to really cut loose. I want you to throw that ball as hard as you can. Make three throws like that, and after each one I'll wrap the ball in some of those old rags over there and throw it back. That way the rain won't sop it up too much." Then I went back to the other barn.

Three times the boy reared back and fired. And each time the catcher would hand me the ball, I'd look it over, then wrap it in some rags and throw it back. After the third pitch I motioned for the catcher to get in the car, told the pitcher I'd seen enough for the time being, and thanked the coach for his help. They climbed into the car and took off. I thanked the farmer for his help and the use of his barns — he seemed to get a kick out of the whole thing — then Gene and I took off too.

We drove for a long time, but neither one of us said anything. Gene seemed to be doing a lot of studying, but he wasn't coming up with any answers. Finally, when I thought he was going to burst, he blurted it out.

"All right, tell me," he said. "What were all those shenanigans back there and just what did you accomplish on this little trip?"

"Take it easy, Gene," I said. "You got to see the boy throw, didn't you?"

"Well, yeah."

"You saw his build, didn't you?"

"Yeah."

"You saw his delivery and pitching motion, didn't you?"

"So?"

"You got to see his fastball, right?"

"Sure. But how could you judge anything under those conditions?"

"I could judge well enough to see that he's not major league material," I said.

"How do you figure?"

"Gene, I'll tell you. That boy threw three of the hardest pitches he could throw, and every time that ball was soaking wet before it even got to the catcher. Any pitcher that can't throw hard enough to get it through that rain and not get a drop on it, I don't want."

Gene laughed so hard I had to pull off the road. And he didn't mind taking that later flight to Florida after all.

Slow, Slower,
Slowest

◆——————————————◆

Tony Lucadello assured that every story and signing in this book was true. Until this one. The following tale is based on fact, but the ending, well it's been stretched a bit. The story is told, however, to bring attention to another piece of Lucadello's past, and to spotlight a man considered the top high school and Acme coach in central Ohio — Lou Brunswick.

I've signed two major leaguers in the same day, but the Brunswicks were the only father-son tandem I ever signed. I landed the father, Lou Brunswick, in 1948, and the son, Tom, around 1965.

I remember one of the last amateur games I saw Tom play, a tournament game in Battle Creek, Michigan. I was hiding behind the rightfield fence, but the Brunswicks saw me. Jeff, the youngest, spotted my houndstooth hat above the fence and tipped off his dad. Lou, who had been coaching both high school and Acme in Coldwater, Ohio, for quite a few years, came out to shake hands and my cover was blown. I didn't mind, because I have as much respect for Lou Brunswick as I do for any coach in the Midwest. Eleven times he's taken his high school or Acme teams to the state tournament, and he's accumulated five state championships. But this story isn't about Lou's teams or his state titles. It's about how I signed him and developed him into the greatest changeup pitcher of all time (pardon my tongue-in-cheek bravado).

I was still scouting with the Cubs back in the '40s and the club had a keen interest in developing its farm system. One of the best ways to man these minor league teams was to hold tryout camps throughout the Midwest, which was my area. Hundreds of potential ballplayers attended the camps; all we had to do was weed out the players we wanted to keep, work them out, and hopefully sign them to a contract.

It was at a tryout camp in Greenville, Ohio, that I first saw Lou Brunswick. Lou's coach at St. Henry High School, Charlie Karcher, was helping me run the camp, so he brought Lou along. I was impressed with Lou from the start. He had a good arm, a nice fluid delivery, and an excellent curve. But his best asset was his control. He was always right around the strike zone. After watching Lou most of the summer, I signed him.

Actually, there were two players I signed out of that Greenville tryout camp. Lou Brunswick was one; Don Elston the other. Both were pitchers, but they were about as alike as night and day. Lou was a mild-mannered farm boy with a lot of talent. Don Elston was a fiery little scamp with more brag than ability. One of the ironies of the game, though, was that Elston went on to become a top reliever for the Cubs, while Lou Brunswick never made the major leagues. I'll tell you what happened.

After signing with the Cubs, Lou was sent to our Class D team in Jamesville, Wisconsin. Lou made the club and was doing fairly well when he injured his arm about midseason. It didn't seem to be too serious of an injury, and by the end of the season Lou was out throwing again. There was a difference, though. Lou felt no pain when he pitched, but he suddenly had no zip on the ball. The injury left him with what's usually called a dead arm.

Lou went home after the season, and shortly he sent me a letter. He said he'd been throwing and the arm felt great, but he wanted me to see for myself. The verdict, however, was the same as before. Lou pitched well when I saw him, but there was nothing on the ball. His control was as good as ever, but his pitches lacked the velocity they once had.

Lou was a good young man and he wanted to stay in baseball. Obviously, he'd have to come up with another pitch, and with his control the changeup seemed the perfect thing. So I showed Lou how to throw the change of pace. I showed him how to grip the ball

and taught him three kinds of changeups: slow, slower, and slowest. Then I told him he'd have to work on his technique all winter
and gave him a good place to start.

"You still milk your cows by hand, don't you?" I asked. And
when he said they did I gave him my plan. "When you're squeez-
ing down on those teats, that's the same grip and motion you'll use
when you're throwing the changeup. Keep that in mind, and work
on it." Then I left.

Lou must have done a lot of milking that winter, because when
spring rolled around he said he was ready. We took him to spring
training and, in one of the exhibition games, we decided to try him
out in relief. There were two outs and Lou had a 2-0 lead when he
took the mound. But the other team had the bases loaded and one
of their big hitters at the plate.

Lou started the guy out with a slow changeup and the hitter, a
little overanxious, pulled it just foul. Then Lou went into a deep
windup and fired his second pitch, a change of pace even slower
than the first. Well out in front of the ball, the hitter again pulled it
foul.

All set for his slowest pitch yet, Lou went into his windup. But
just as he did so, the runners took off. The man on third scored
standing up. So did the man on second. And just as the runner from
first slid in safely, the umpire yelled strike three. Lou had struck
the batter out, but he still lost 3-2.

Well, maybe that's not really what happened, at least the last
part anyway. But it's been a running joke between Lou and me.
Maybe it's my way of evening things a little. Lou always said I
signed him for a bag of peanuts and a bottle of pop, and calls me an
old penny-pincher because I like to walk around a ballfield looking for loose change. Well, maybe his contract wasn't that big, and
so I like to keep my nose to the ground. Looking for loose change is
how I get my exercise between games, and you never walk past a
penny. It's a sure sign of luck.

Lou Brunswick could have used a lucky penny when he suf-
fered that arm injury. I thought he could have played major league
ball.

Don Elston didn't need much luck, though. What he got he
earned through dedication, determination, and desire.

I didn't even want to sign Don Elston when I first saw him at
a tryout camp in Mansfield. He was small and skinny and I wasn't

too impressed with his side-arm style of pitching. All the players at these camps filled out cards after the workout, and if I was interested in a boy I'd use that card to keep in touch with him. But Elston, after that tryout in Mansfield, approached me right afterward and said he had to know right away what I thought. He said he'd come a long way to attend that camp and wouldn't go home without an answer. I was straightforward with him. I told him I didn't think he had major league potential, but if he wanted he could come to our next tryout at Greenville and I'd give him another chance.

When I left I thought that was the last I'd seen of Don Elston. But suddenly I started getting letters from the boy, at least one every day. His notes were short, usually about how he was working hard and looking forward to the next camp. And day after day, week after week, they kept coming in like clockwork. I saw Don Elston again at the Greenville camp, but wasn't any more impressed than the first time I'd seen him.

The whole matter might have ended there except for a set of circumstances that fall. In September there was a minor league convention in Buffalo, New York, and Jack Sheehan wanted me to go with him. We boarded a train in Toledo, and during the long ride to New York I mentioned Don Elston and how he'd come to the camps and written me every day in between.

Jack chuckled when he heard that and said, "If I was you, Tony, I'd sign that boy. That kind of enthusiasm could be a real plus in our program."

So I ended up signing Don Elston, though not for much. He went to Jamesville with Lou Brunswick, but he didn't make a name for himself until very late in the season. Jamesville had a big manager named Jim Oglesbee — Diamond Jim, he was called. With four games left in the season Jamesville was in last place, but Big Jim said if the team won two of those last four games it would sure help his chances of keeping the job another season. That's when that fiery side of Don Elston spoke up.

"If you'd pitch the right people we'll win two out of four," he said.

"I suppose you mean you," Jim hollered back.

"Damn right," Elston said, and he got his way. He pitched two of the last four games and won them both.

Despite his late-season theatrics, Elston did not have a spot wrapped up in our organization. But our rule was that any player who played one full year in the minor leagues got invited to spring training the following year. Elston had a free ride to our training camp in Moltree, Georgia, but from there he earned everything on his own.

Elston did everything to make the team. He got up early and polished the other players' shoes, hung out the bats, and swept the locker room. When the managers held their meeting to decide who they'd keep and who would be let go, Elston was one of the five extra players allowed to stay on the roster an extra thirty days. Don used that time to his advantage, doing everything from lining the fields to driving the bus. Before you knew it, it was time to assign him to a minor league team (because he was still on the roster) and Don's opportunity had come. He won fifteen or sixteen games with Sioux Falls, then survived a near fatal appendicitis attack the following year. That was when I really got to know Don Elston. His parents had no phone, and there was no way to contact them when he had the attack. So I signed for him at the hospital and stayed with him four or five days.

Don Elston bounced back to become one of the Cubs' top relievers, leading the majors with sixty-nine appearances in 1958 and tying teammate Bill Henry for the most appearances in the National League the following season with sixty-five. Not bad for a skinny little kid who bugged the hell out of me until I signed him.

The Three "P"s
of Scouting

◆————————————————◆

Schoolin' and scoutin' have a lot in common. To get an education
you study the basics — readin', 'ritin', and 'rithmetic. It's the same
with scoutin', only instead of the three "R"s you use one of the
three "P"s — projection, performance, or picking.

Basically, there are four kinds of scouts: (1) the super scout,
who keeps tabs on the major leaguers and acts as an advance scout
for the big league club; (2) the scout whose job it is to keep an eye
on the development and talent in the minor leagues; (3) the cross-
checker, who compares the talent in different areas to see which is
the best draft choice for a team; and (4) the area scouts, who ferret
out the raw talent in one specific territory.

I'm an area scout, among the ones I consider the foundation of
the system. It's our job to uncover the budding talent we feel has
major league potential. It's not the easiest job, or the most successful. If we're fifty percent right, that's about the ultimate. If you hit
fifty percent you're doing an excellent job for your club. If you sign
two players and one makes it to the major leagues, or sign four and
two make it, that's outstanding. I feel I've done a little better than
that, somewhere between fifty-five and sixty percent. But that's because when I see a young ballplayer, I try to project what he can

be. That's what separates me from the performance scouts and the pickers.

I can always spot the performance scouts and pickers at a ballgame. They're usually sitting right behind home plate — the performance scouts because all they're interested in is whether a boy will get three hits or strike out twenty batters, and the pickers because they need someone to bitch to.

Performance scouts just wait for something to happen. If a ballplayer has a good day, if he hits well, throws well, and fields his position well, then he is judged on his performance and little else. The scout sees the boy run, but he can't get an accurate impression from up in the stands. He sees the boy throw, but he makes his decisions on balls and strikes and putouts instead of motion, technique, accuracy, and velocity.

Performance scouts usually recommend a ballplayer only on his statistics. Because a boy had a bad day, though, they often eliminate the best overall ballplayer in the bunch.

Pickers are just perfectionists in disguise. Instead of looking for the good points, they pick on a ballplayer's weakness. This one can't hit, they'll say, or that one hasn't got the range. A picker will pounce on a minor detail, something that possibly could be corrected with a little work, and overlook the things a ballplayer may do well. Sure, a picker might find that perfect ballplayer and sign him. But in the process he might overlook ten players with the potential to be major leaguers.

That's why projection is a crucial part of my success as a baseball scout. I can't just look at what a young man has done; I have to visualize what he can do.

My projection system isn't foolproof. It didn't work too well with Pete Rose. Joe Hawk was after me for a long time to sign the little second baseman from Western Hills, but I said he was too small to make it big. Unfortunately, I didn't project two things: the size of the man's heart and his unquenchable desire to excel.

Fergie Jenkins, Grant Jackson, and Toby Harrah seem to have done all right, even if I do say so myself. All three were scouted through the simple process of projection.

It's not all that simple, really, as many of my fellow scouts who have seen me skittering all over the ball diamonds of the Midwest can attest. Projection scouting involves getting all the information you can. You have to if you're to try and project a ballplayer you see on the sandlots as a major leaguer. Certain areas of the field and certain areas of the body are used in my projection scouting, but I have to go beyond that. I also have to consider whether a boy really wants to play baseball, what his background is, whether he will work hard enough to succeed, and whether he has the desire, dedication, and determination to push himself.

Basically, there are eight positions on the field and eight areas of the body I take into consideration when I seriously scout a player I'm interested in. There are three positions down each foul line that I scout from: the first about ten feet down either line (but far enough back to be out of the way), the second behind first base and third base, and the third about halfway out to the outfield. The other two positions are beyond the outfield fence, at the points between the outfielders. The eight parts of the body are the upper half and lower half (front and back), and left side and right side (front and back). Depending on who I'm scouting, whether it be a pitcher, thirdbaseman, or outfielder, these positions and areas are critical. You'd be surprised at the difference you see in a ballplayer from one angle to another. It can affect your whole perspective and ultimately your overall projection. From one angle you might notice a weakness you didn't see before. Then, after you've seen a ballplayer from all sides, you determine whether that weakness can be corrected with added strength or a change in technique. It's a decision I could never make by sitting in the stands.

Each position on the field is important, but the first one, about ten feet down the line, is, I feel, the key spot. If I'm really interested in a ballplayer, one I think has major league potential, I want to see his face, especially his eyes, when he's up at the plate. If someone asked me what's the key I look at most when I'm scouting, I'd say the face. The face can fill in the intangibles no batting average or pitching record ever can. It will tell me whether a ballplayer really loves the game, whether he's aggressive or not, and whether he has the desire to go with his ability. The face tells me if a hitter is stiff or relaxed, whether a pitcher is confident in his pitches or has doubts. It's all there right in front of me.

That first position also gives me all the technical information I need. I can see the front of the hitter (or the back half if he's left-handed) so I know how he holds his hands, how he moves his feet, and how the bat crosses his body. The pitcher is also right in front of me so I get the full view of his motion and immediately know what his ball does — whether it moves or is flat, whether his fastball sinks or his curve hangs. I can see the catcher and his actions and the front view of the infielders.

From the thirdbase side I get the opposite view of righthanded hitters and lefthanded pitchers. Down the line farther I check out the infielders' throws across the field, the back of the pitcher and the front of the outfielders. Each position has its own advantage, but each is also just one segment of the entire picture.

When I leave a ballfield, I know I've had a good, complete look at the ballplayer I'd come to see. I know I'm in a better position to project how high that ballplayer can go and, more importantly, evaluate how much money he is worth for us to sign him. How a performance scout or picker could make that judgment by sitting in the stands I'll never know.

Although projection involves all areas of the body, I pay particular attention to the lower half of the anatomy. I've scouted a lot of years and I've come to the conclusion that eighty-seven percent of the game of baseball is played from the waist down. Other sports vary. In basketball, for instance, the upper half of the body may command ninety to ninety-five percent of the game, while in golf the lower half is almost all of the sport.

Baseball isn't dominated as much as golf by the lower half of the body, but the eighty-seven percent figure seems appropriate. More grounders than fly balls are fielded and a player has to get down and have the good defensive stance. Pitchers always try to spot the ball between the knees and the belt, so again you're dealing with the lower half of the body. Then, of course, there's the running and footwork.

Technically speaking, I judge a ballplayer on four major factors: his speed, his arm, his hands, and his ability with the bat. To complete my projection, though, I have to also consider a boy's background, character, and commitment. When I've weighed all the information and I'm still sold on a ballplayer, then I give the front office an estimate of what I'd offer the prospect if we were to draft him.

That's not the end of it. The next move is to bring in a crosschecker, a scout who will compare my recommendation against, say, another prospect halfway across the country. His decision could well decide whether we draft a player in the second or third round, or whether we draft him at all.

It's a tough job for the cross-checker, especially in my area, the Midwest. Spring can be a fickle season with cold Aprils and wet Mays. A team might play two solid weeks in beautiful sunshine, then not get back on the ball diamond the rest of the month.

Some ballplayers don't find their groove until late May or early June. And if it's getting close to the draft and we're pushing the deadline, a cross-checker may have to make his recommendation on performance, or a combination of performance and projection. The key there remains the word "performance." If a player has a bad day the cross-checker may not like him and consequently won't recommend him to the front office. Personally, that's why I feel most farm directors should take into consideration the area scout recommending a ballplayer and his past reputation. After all, the heart of area scouting is covering the sandlot programs in the summertime — the Acme, American Legion, and amateur ranks. Area scouts see the players under all conditions, both good and bad, and that's where we have the advantage. I think most farm directors and cross-checkers realize that, especially if they're dealing with a scout with a lot of experience and a respected reputation.

I feel I've been successful, thanks to the contacts I made along the way. I've found my share of good ballplayers, but I also latched onto a bunch more through tips from high school, college, and sandlot coaches.

But I never realized how much weight my scouting carried until I learned other major league scouts were scouting me. Several coaches have told me scouts have asked them if Lucadello had been snooping around and wondered who I was after. It's flattering, in a way. I wonder what method they're using — projection, performance, or picking. Hopefully, it's not the fourth "P" of the business — poor scouting.

Super Scouts

◆————————————————————————◆

Many of the ballplayers Tony Lucadello signed are already established superstars. Several more probably will be in the future.

Barry Bonnell, for example, had an excellent year with the Toronto Blue Jays and Jim Essian had a banner season with the Seattle Mariners in 1982. Though both were signed by Lucadello, neither remained with the Phillies organization long. To understand why these two promising young players were traded, you have to consider the role of one of the key figures in major league baseball — the Super Scout.

Signing Barry Bonnell was relatively easy; signing Jim Essian took a bit more effort on my part. But I signed them both, and though they're not with the Phillies now, Barry Bonnell and Jim Essian were key figures in a major trade, the type of trade Super Scouts are expected to make in big league wheeling and dealing.

Just outside Cincinnati, Barry Bonnell played and starred for Millford High School. The Chicago White Sox drafted him upon graduation, but he didn't sign with them. Barry had a scholarship to attend Ohio State and thought he'd test the college ranks first.

Two years later, though, Barry took himself out of school to make himself eligible for the January draft. According to the rule, he had to be out of school at least 125 days to qualify for entry.

When we saw his name on the eligibility list, we planned on making him our number-one pick. We had been high on Barry for quite some time and, since we had the first pick that year, we were confident we could sign him.

Actually, there were two ballplayers in my area I rated very high. Barry Bonnell was one, Dave Tobik was the other. But when the front office called me and asked which of the two I liked best, I said I'd have to take Bonnell.

Fortunately, I got a chance to back up my statement before the draft. Barry played for the Pan American team in Florida and several of our front office people got to see him play during our annual meeting down there. Dallas Green, our farm director then, and Hugh Alexander, one of our Super Scouts, were especially impressed. Backed by their support, I signed him.

The Detroit Tigers picked right after us in the draft and they took Dave Tobik. He's now one of the top relief pitchers on their staff.

Signing Jim Essian was different. It took excellent cooperation, great timing, and the help of a dear friend of mine, Ed Finau, a legend of the Detroit sandlots. He's been a scorekeeper for the amateur teams for at least thirty years.

Jim Essian was an outstanding athlete. He was offered a scholarship to Michigan, and you have to be good to get a free ride there. But the June draft came and went, and Jim wasn't drafted. All that was left, at least for the time being, was to play sandlot ball in the amateur leagues of Detroit.

It was there that one of my scouts, Casey Lopata, noticed Jim Essian and told me about him. "You'd better come up and see him," Casey said, " 'cause everyone else is."

So I checked the kid out and really liked what I saw. Jim had a great talent, and he seemed to get better and better every time I saw him. But Jim was also getting an awful lot of attention from several other ball clubs. And, since he hadn't been selected in the June draft, he was virtually a free agent and in a position to deal for himself. It looked as if I was on the outs, coming in late and not as well prepared as the other scouts.

Then I remembered Ed Finau, the scorekeeper with the amazing memory who was always ready with the jokes. I had known Ed for quite some time and knew that if he could he would do anything for anybody.

"Ed," I said, calling him over, "I want you to do me a favor. I want you to sit by Jim Essian while you keep the book and tell him to be sure and be home at nine o'clock. Tell him he's going to get a very important phone call at that time. Don't tell him who's calling. I don't want to tip my hand. I don't want anyone to know I'm even interested in the boy. If you do me this one favor, I'll give you $100."

Ed relayed the message, as I knew he would. And later in my hotel room, at nine o'clock, I made the call.

"Jim," I said, "how would you like to fly to Philadelphia tomorrow and try out with the Phillies?"

"You mean that?" he asked, a bit skeptical.

"Every word," I said. "There's a plane leaving at nine in the morning and I've got reservations for you. Someone from our office will pick you up in Philadelphia, you can work out with the team, stick around for the afternoon game, catch an early flight back, and be back in Detroit by nine tomorrow night. What do you say?"

Needless to say, Jim jumped at the chance. Early next morning I picked him up personally, so we could get acquainted, and put him on the plane. Everything had already been cleared with the front office, so the plan went smoothly. Late in the afternoon, when Jim had had his workout and been put on the return flight home, I got a call from Robert Carpenter himself.

"Tony, you have to sign that kid," he said. "He proved to us he's all you said he was. We have to have him."

"I'll sign him," I said. And later that night, after I'd picked Jim up at the airport and taken him home, I did just that.

I'm pretty proud of that deal because of the way everything worked out. We all get beat sometimes; that's the name of the game. I was a bit lucky too. I knew I had to work fast, so I set up a plan and it worked. The key was that it all went so smoothly, thanks to the cooperation of the people in the front office.

The fact that I'd signed Jim Essian, though, did not set well with everyone. The following night I was out at Tiger Stadium and obviously news of the signing had leaked out. From my seat I could see some Tigers officials in a heated discussion, and by the way they were looking and pointing I knew it was about me. Finally, one of them got up and came to where I was sitting.

"Damnit, Tony," he said. "I just caught hell because you signed Jim Essian right under our noses. But it's like the boss said, if someone was going to get him, it'd probably be you."

That basically ended my role in the signings, but Barry Bonnell and Jim Essian would figure in a greater scheme for the Phillies. It came in 1975 when both were part of a trade that brought us Richie Allen.

We knew Bonnell and Essian were future talents, but you have to take into consideration the fact that we thought we could win the pennant and possibly the World Series with Richie Allen's power in the lineup. We felt we had to gamble somewhere, but that's what you have to do in this business. In order to fill one certain spot that might win you all the marbles, you sometimes have to sacrifice young players who have talent but who couldn't step right onto a major league team that's chasing a pennant. That's why trades are made, and that's why there are men like Hugh Alexander — the Super Scouts, we call them.

I'm not a Super Scout; I'm an area scout. I beat the bushes for raw talent that forms the foundation for the minor and major league systems.

A Super Scout is the right arm of the general manager. He's involved in trades — almost always on the major league level — and serves as an advance scout for the parent club. It's his job to find out who's hitting and who's not, who's pitching well and who's in a slump, what pitch a guy chases in a particular situation, whether a runner prefers to steal on the second pitch or the third. These little things can mean a slight edge between winning and losing. It's a tough job. They live on airplanes and out of suitcases.

The biggest role of a Super Scout keys on the trades. He has to be pretty accurate in regards to whether a particular ballplayer can help a team immediately. And if that established player can step right in and produce right off the bat, the question would be is he worth, say, two promising young players who would be a nucleus for the future.

Sometimes a Super Scout has to stick his neck out, but that's part of his job. He's dealing with the high rollers of the game, the players who are making $400,000-$500,000 a year or more, and there's an awful lot riding on his decisions.

The Spoils of Scouting:
The Signing of George Williams

◆────────────────────◆

The various methods of scouting Tony Lucadello has used in his long and storied career have been imaginative, to say the least. They've been highly successful, to say the most.

Though the institution of the draft system initiated a new style of scouting, one got the impression that Lucadello preferred the old days when commitment and dedication to the sport meant more to a prospect than a huge signing bonus. It was a time when a scout wined-and-dined and got close to the player and his family.

But it was also a time of shady deals and backroom contracts. It wasn't unusual for a player to be pressured into signing with a certain team, or bootlegged away from another. Lucadello didn't favor that kind of scouting, but sometimes he just couldn't avoid it.

I signed a player out of Detroit back in the '50s, a player named George Williams. George was an infielder, a second baseman, and I'd scouted him often on the sandlots of Detroit. Eventually, George made it to the major leagues, but he didn't play long, only fifty or sixty games in the three years he was with Philadelphia, Houston, and Kansas City.

But this story is about the signing of George Williams, and some of the shadier aspects of scouting.

The first time I approached George and said I wanted to sign him he turned me down. He said he wanted to think about it awhile and play sandlot in the meantime. But a few weeks later I got a call from George saying he was ready to listen to my offer. George said there were only two teams he was interested in playing for — ours and another team I'd rather not mention — and that he would listen to offers from both. The other team's scout was to be at his house at seven that night. I was to be allowed to talk to George at eight.

I was a bit surprised at the sudden turnaround. But I found out later that George's mother had been sick and needed an operation. I think the family needed the signing bonus George would get to cover the hospital bills.

Later that day I drove to Detroit. When I pulled up in front of George's house I saw the car of another scout there. I could tell who it was by the sticker in the back window. I wasn't worried, though. I knew I was a little early, so I settled back and waited.

Eight o'clock came and I was getting my things together, but the other scout was still inside the house. Fifteen minutes passed, then half an hour, and he still hadn't come out. Pretty soon it was close to nine and I was upset. I was just getting ready to go up to the house when Joe Jackson came along. Joe carried a lot of weight in the Detroit sandlot programs back then. He had coached the team George played on and I had dealt with him in the past. We were pretty good friends, and he'd come along to see me talk to George.

"What's up, Tony?" he said when he got near my car.

"I'm not sure," I told him. "I was supposed to talk to George at eight, but the other scout has been in there all night. I'm getting concerned. I'm afraid they'll get to him and sign George before I even have a chance to make an offer."

Joe, I could see, didn't appreciate it either.

"Tell you what, Tony," he said. "Drive around behind the house and pull through the alley. I'll take care of things from here."

I didn't know what Joe had planned, but I did as he asked. I circled the block, pulled up behind the house, and doused my lights. About ten minutes later the back door opened and out came George, his parents, and Joe. Joe put the rest in the back, then jumped up front with me and said, "Let's go."

Joe took us all over to his house and I made my offer to George

Williams. He thought it over for a while, discussed it with his parents, and signed the contract.

On the way back to George's house, Joe explained what happened earlier. He had confronted the other scout, asking what he was doing there so long and telling him there was another scout waiting outside. The scout told him he was just doing his job, trying to sign a ballplayer his team wanted badly. Joe told him he had to talk it over with George and his parents. But instead of taking them into another room Joe marched them into the kitchen, out the back door, and right into my car.

George got the money his mother needed for the operation, but I don't agree with the way we had to sneak around and get the contract signed. Sometimes, though, you're left with no other choice. I wouldn't have handled it like that if there had been any other way. I guess that goes back even to the days I was playing minor league ball myself. I was a cocky little so-and-so, but I had to be. As small as I was, I was an easy target. But I wasn't going to let anyone push me around. I didn't go looking for trouble, but if somebody started messing with me I wasn't going to back down.

I think that attitude carried over into my scouting. The George Williams incident, however, was nothing compared to one I'd had earlier. That one involved outright kidnapping.

I'm not going to mention names and places. The incident happened long ago, and as far as I'm concerned it's over. I had a promising young player from Northwest Ohio ready to sign, but when I went to his house he was gone. No one knew where he was, not even his mother.

I found out later that another scout had told the boy I wasn't interested in him, and that I wasn't going to offer him a contract. My web of contacts told me this scout had shown up at the boy's house and driven off with him early in the day.

I knew which direction they were headed, though, and took off after them. I found them at a motel just across the state line late that night. I went to the boy's room and told him what was going on. He thought the other scout was taking him to a tryout camp. I put him in my car and drove him home. I re-kidnapped him, I guess you could say.

That kind of thing doesn't happen anymore. But in a way I miss that mystery and intrigue of the old days. It wasn't always legal, but it sure was fun.

Underground Hound

I once wanted to check out a ballplayer in West Frankfort, Illinois. He had graduated from high school the year before and was working in the coal mines there. There were four mines in West Frankfort — one, two, three, and four. My dad worked in number four; this kid worked in number three mine.

The boy wasn't playing for any team at the time, so I figured I'd have to work him out somewhere near the mines. But this place had no facilities whatsoever. No gym or anything.

I was hoping I could work him out somewhere outside, but when I went down to see him it was raining. Three days I hung around trying to see this kid and for three days it just rained, rained, rained.

I was covering seven states at the time and had already wasted three days trying to see one ballplayer. I had other places to check, more ballplayers to scout. But it just kept on raining.

Finally, I decided that if it rained the next day I was still going to see this kid pitch somehow. The next day, as usual, it rained.

So I went up to the mine, up to the head shed, and talked to the man in charge. I explained the situation to him and asked if there was any way I could get into the mine to see this kid. As luck would have it, this kid's brother, a catcher, also worked in the

127

mines and I was hoping I could use that to my advantage.

"I'll be happy to help," the guy says. "I can get him and his brother together. And there's a few other guys I can spare for a half hour or so if you need them."

That was music to my ears. I got my gear out of the car — a catcher's mitt, some baseballs, and an infielder's glove I carried around just in case. Back at the shed, the foreman put me on an elevator and down I went to the level this kid was working on — 300 feet underground.

The foreman must have called ahead because a bunch of men were waiting on me when I reached their level. I told them what I had in mind and passed out the equipment.

There was no trouble lining up the pitcher and catcher. Railroad tracks that they used for coal carts ran straight down the shafts, so I just stood the catcher in one place and the pitcher about sixty feet farther down. Then I took some of the miners standing around and put four of them right behind the catcher so their headlamps would shine just in front of him. That way he could see the ball coming in.

I put two others between home plate and the pitcher, so they could follow the path of the ball, and three others around the pitcher — one behind him and one on each side so he could see the return throw.

That's the way I worked out a pitcher in West Frankfort, 300 feet down in a coal mine. I had him throw for about thirty minutes, checking his speed, his delivery, his body movement, and his style.

When he was finished, I thanked the miners for their help, took the elevator back up the shaft, jumped into my car, and drove off. The kid wasn't a prospect; he couldn't throw hard enough. But I figured if I wanted to be a good scout, sometimes I'd have to dig a little deeper and try a little harder than the next man to see all the talent I could — no matter where or when.

Climb Every Mountain

◆————————————◆

Back in the early '50s, when I was still working with the Cubs, I heard about a pitcher named Smith somewhere around Glasglow, Kentucky. He was reported to be outstanding, but that was all the information I had.

So I drove down to Glasglow and inquired around until I located somebody who knew the boy. He said the kid lived near Hiseville, not too far away, and pointed me in the right direction.

"It's just a couple mile," he said. "Just follow this here road."

It may have been a couple of miles — about six, he told me — but it took me over two hours to get there. This was in the backwoods of Kentucky, with twisting, turning, winding roads I had never seen before and hope never to see again. I got fouled up so many times I didn't know which road to take. So I took them all.

Finally, I found the place, a tiny little burg out in the middle of nowhere. I started asking around again and found out he worked on a farm about two miles outside of town.

"It's just a couple mile," the fellow said. "Just follow that there road."

I should have walked.

I found the farm, a few more hours later. And there, plowing the ground behind a team of sweaty horses, was the pitcher I'd come all that way to see. I watched for a while, but didn't see a whole lot of him. This whole area was mounds; mounds and hills that rolled all over the place. The kid would pop up coming over one hill, then disappear over another. I doubt there was sixty feet of flat land anywhere in that county.

Eventually, I got the boy's attention, after yelling myself half silly, and he came over to the car.

"You the boy who pitches for a team in Hiseville?" I asked.

"Yeah."

"Well, I'm Tony Lucadello. I scout for the Chicago Cubs. And I came down to look at you."

"Where?"

"Well, I'll tell you," I said. "I had one heckuva time getting down here and I'll be darned if I'm going to drive back or take you back somewhere where I can work you out where the field is better. I've got all the equipment we need in the car, so if you're game I'll try you out right here."

"Sure. Anytime a scout comes down to see me, I'm willing to throw."

We went to the back of my car and I got out a catcher's mitt and gave him a couple of baseballs. Then I took off my shoes, rolled up my pants' legs, and set about looking for some place we could throw.

We were almost at the base of the mountains. Most of the hills were just little knobs, but a few had some gentle slope to them. Finally, I found a place that wasn't too bad. There was a dip between two hills with a creek running through the middle. I positioned him on one hill and I took the other. His wasn't bad. It tapered down just like a pitching mound. But I felt like I was sitting on the side of a mountain.

I let him get warmed up for twenty or thirty minutes. Then I told him to bear down and burn it. About ten minutes later I said I'd seen enough, walked back to the car, and put the equipment away.

"I hate to tell you this, son," I told him. "But I just don't think you're ready yet. Maybe I can catch you again under better conditions."

I thought that was that, and drove away. But a few days later, I got a call from my office.

"Did you work out a youngster named Smith in Hiseville, Kentucky?" they asked.

I said sure.

"Well, his sister lives right near Wrigley Field," they told me, "and she came storming in here saying you didn't give the kid a fair chance. She said you made him work off of a hill. Is that true?"

I told them it wasn't exactly a hill. It was more like a mound, a pitching mound. And I explained about the area, that there wasn't any smooth ground to work him on. And I told them that because of the trouble I had getting to him in the first place I wasn't going to leave without seeing whether the kid had a good arm, a good body, and what I was looking for in a major leaguer. The kid had a good body — he was about six-foot and 170 pounds. But he didn't have a good delivery and he didn't throw hard enough.

So they asked me what I was going to do and I said, "Hey, I'm not going back to look at him again. I didn't like him the first time. He isn't going to show me any more if I took him out onto Wrigley Field and worked him out where it's nice and flat. I'm convinced he's not a pro prospect."

Unknown to me, though, the kid was invited to Wrigley Field a short time later. He stayed with his sister, the one who seemed to have started this whole thing. And Charlie Grimm, the Cubs manager then, liked the kid and signed him to a contract.

So now they send the kid to spring training in Moultrie, Georgia, and it just so happens that I'm in charge of the Moultrie camp. He went through spring training, but when it came time to do some cutting, he was one of the first to go. I didn't like what I saw; neither did the manager. So we sent him home.

I thought that ended it for good. But a few days later my office gets on the horn again.

"Why'd you release that kid?" they asked.

"For the same reason I told you I didn't want him when I drove through all those backwoods hills to see him in Hiseville," I told them.

They got pretty upset at that. They even sent another guy down to Hiseville to see the kid again. He came back and said the same thing I did. The kid just wasn't major league potential.

I tried to tell them.

Half a Home Run is Better Than None

◆——————————————◆

I was working with the Cubs back in the early '50s when the front office called with an assignment. A good-looking young infielder was going to be playing his final game of the season the following Sunday, and they wanted me to check him out. The boy came highly recommended by a former major leaguer, and the front office felt his recommendation was worthwhile.

So I packed up the car and got ready to head for Alamo, Indiana. But when I checked the map I couldn't find the place. It wasn't even listed. I finally had to call Indianapolis and talk to some state department people about where this little burg was. They gave me directions, but I was a bit leery as I started out.

Persistence and the grace of God steered me over the tiny Indiana backroads, though, and near noon the following Sunday I pulled into Alamo. Bumped into it, was more like it. A general store, gas station, and luncheonette were about all the town had worth mentioning. The store was the only place that looked open.

"There a ballgame here today?" I asked after I'd introduced myself to the shopkeeper.

"Yeah. About one-thirty," he said. "Who you come to see?"

I told him, and like most storekeepers this man knew everyone in town. "He's a good one," he said. "He's about nineteen now, but he's been one of the best ballplayers in the area for years."

"I'll judge that myself," I said. "By the way, where's the ball-park? I haven't seen anything but this store and the few buildings around it."

"Tell you what," the man said. "I'll get you a guide. It's kinda hard to find, being on the other side of the woods and all. But my boy's going to the game and he can ride along with you. I was going myself later on, and I can just pick him up there."

That was fine by me. So he called to his son, a young boy of twelve or thirteen, and off we went. It was good I had him along. I'd have never found the field if he wasn't. We pulled off the town's main street onto a dirt road and for almost a mile drove through heavy woods, with the trees so close on either side the branches kept scraping the fenders of the car.

Suddenly, we came out into the open and there, right in the middle of a little valley, was the ballfield. It wasn't a fancy ball-park, but it looked neat and well kept. There were bleachers for about fifty people (which, I think, was half the town's total popu-lation) and already the stands were half-filled. It was a lighted dia-mond, which amazed me for a town that size, and I noticed that some of the power lines hung down over the outfield, especially in left and right.

I had just located the player I'd come to see when something else shocked me — these guys were throwing around a softball, not a baseball. I questioned some of the people there and learned the regular baseball season had ended the week before. At the end of the summer, though, the best players in the area got together for a benefit fast-pitch softball game.

I thought about packing up and heading home but figured, hell, I was there anyway. And the boy I wanted to see was going to be playing third. At least I'd get an indication of how he threw, how he handled himself on the field, and whether he had the size and speed of a prospect.

I had just settled back in my seat when the umpire — Abe Lin-coln in overalls — stepped onto the field. He was a tall man, six-foot-five at least, straight as an arrow and with a beard. What struck me was the aura of power that surrounded him. He was so straight, so aloof. No one questioned him or talked to him. He just stood there looking straight ahead, saying nothing. He had on red shin guards and one of those long belly protectors that went all the way to the knees. That's how they were made back then. He had an iron mask in one hand, and there was a rule book sticking out the back pocket of his overalls.

I switched my attention to the ballplayer when the game started. He had a good, accurate arm and moved his feet well. He fielded his position well, but it was hard to make any determination since he was playing softball.

My interest, though, kept going back to the umpire. I've seen major league umpires have less command of a game than that man. He called balls and strikes with such authority that his word was law. No one dared question anything he said or did. For all the respect and dignity he received, he might have been a minister or a sheriff. Apparently, he was a powerful man in the community with a great amount of influence.

Inning after inning umpire Abe barked out his calls. No one ever disputed his decision or argued a call. So it came to the last half of the ninth inning, the score tied 1-1, and the boy I'd come to see stepped up to the plate.

A big strong boy he was. And on the very first pitch he put every ounce of muscle and bone into a vicious line drive that shot off his bat like a rocket. Necks almost cracked as the ball cleared the infield, still rising. Without a doubt it would clear the fence with room to spare.

Fate, though, had other plans. That screaming liner hit one of the power lines directly and was sheared right in half. The top half kept sailing, right over the fence. The lower half fluttered to the ground where the leftfielder retrieved it and sort of frisbeed it to second, holding the hitter to a double.

The crowd buzzed and the players looked confused, but the umpire never hesitated. Tall and straight, that grim look cemented on his face, he strode to the mound, waved the runner to third, then to home.

A murmur rustled across the diamond, but the umpire held up his arms and all went quiet.

"Ladies and gentlemen," he said, pulling the rule book from his pocket, "here is my rule book. There is no rule in it to cover the event you have just seen. No rule whatsoever.

"We do have a field rule that states if a ball hits the wires and goes over the fence, it's a home run. If it hits the wires and remains in play, the runner can take as many bases as he can. But in this particular case, where half the ball went over the fence and half stayed on the playing field, I have to make a ruling as the umpire in chief. I rule that it counts as half a home run and, therefore, the home team wins one-and-a-half to one."

And that's exactly how the game ended.

Harrumphs
For the Umps

◆————————————————————◆

Tony Lucadello saw some amazing things in his forty-plus years of scouting. Some were exciting, some terrifying, some just flat-out hilarious. A good deal of the lighter moments of Tony's exploits have involved the harried and hassled men in blue, the umpires. Fittingly, it is to their memory that we set aside a small portion of this book.

I like umpires, I really do. Many times when I was on the road scouting major league teams I stayed at the same hotel as the umpires did and I became good friends with several of them. We'd sit around the lobby and swap tales or compare ballplayers, just like a bunch of old hens.

I realized umpires took more than their share of abuse. Some of it may have been warranted; most of it wasn't. But any man who dons the blue knows that he's going to be a target for all sorts of verbal lambasting. It goes with the job.

I've seen my share of bad calls in my day, but there was one call, the one I consider the greatest decision ever made by an umpire, that outweighs any misconceptions I ever had for the profession. It didn't occur in the major leagues. Surprisingly, it wasn't even in professional baseball of any kind. It occurred in an American Legion game between two small-town Michigan rivals — Edwardsburg and Niles — on July 7, 1952.

Edwardsburg and Niles, you've got to understand, aren't baseball heaven. Compared to Detroit, Dayton, and Cleveland, they're just flyspecks on the map. They played good ball, though. Darn good ball. And because the towns were only ten or twelve miles apart, there was a rivalry between Edwardsburg and Niles that was like nothing else. When you get friends and neighbors and uncles and cousins battling for bragging rights like these two towns did, nothing — and I mean nothing — had better get in the way.

Edwardsburg had an oufielder I was interested in, a big strapping kid who could hit it a ton. I decided to drive on up and look him over good.

I remember it was hot the morning I took off, unbearably hot, it seemed, for so early in the day. And it didn't get any better the farther north I got. When I hit Edwardsburg the place was a furnace. The game was supposed to start at two and by early afternoon you knew you were in for a scorcher. Heat waves rippled up from the pavement and the air was so heavy you felt like someone was holding a big pillow over the whole area, trying to smother everyone underneath.

There had been a number of bad storms already that summer and the conditions were perfect for another. Sure enough, just about game time, you could notice a darkening way off in the west. Gradually, it grew and spread, but it caused only a casual stir among the crowd. The storm was still miles off, and Edwardsburg and Niles were locked in one of their classic struggles. Edwardsburg had scored a run in the bottom of the first inning, but Niles had hung tough with good defense and pitching and finally tied it 1-1 with a run in the fourth.

Everyone was so wrapped up in the game that they forgot about the weather. But I remember looking west after the fourth inning and I was amazed at what I saw. The game was played on what they used to call a town field, not a big ballpark or anything, and it was out in the open. And straight west of it was an ugly mountain of black. That little smokelike darkness I had seen earlier had mushroomed into a seething thunderhead. Sunshine still lingered over the field, but off to the west it was as if someone had pulled a curtain of pure black.

Even then I felt the first cold wind of the storm. The fans felt it, too, but most just glanced over their shoulders and stayed where they were. They probably would have stuck it out had the policeman not come by in the fifth inning. He pulled up to the park, announced over his loudspeaker that a tornado had been sighted coming this way, and urged everyone to vacate the area. People then left in droves, piling into their cars and taking off.

I was about to leave, too, when I noticed the players still on the field. Come hell or high water they were going to finish their game. I took one quick look at the storm, now barreling in like a freight train, and sat back down.

The sixth inning came and went, and the tempest rolled closer. A brooding darkness now covered the entire field and the wind began to gust, knocking hats off players' heads and sending tiny twisters dancing across the infield.

Niles failed to score in the top of the seventh. And, with the storm ready to cut loose any minute, Edwardsburg came to bat.

The first batter grounded out, but the second walked and stole second. The third popped harmlessly to second, and up stepped the big outfielder I'd come to see.

There were no spectators left except me, the players, the umpire, and the storm, which seemed to hang above us waiting until the final out to cut loose.

The batter, figuring the storm could break any second, swung at the first pitch, a curve up and away. He got it all, but not the way he wanted. Instead of a clean single or booming home run, he got under it and hit a towering fly ball. Higher and higher it climbed, held up by the stiff winds, until it was just a tiny white speck against the blackness of the sky. The centerfielder came in; the second baseman and shortstop went out. All had a chance of catching the ball. Buffeted by the winds, the ball hung for a split second, then slowly started to fall.

Suddenly, a blinding flash split the sky and a thundering boom shook the ground. Scared nearly out of my wits, I saw the storm's first lightning bolt strike the ball and blow it into three pieces.

The Niles players quickly recovered from the shock. The centerfielder caught one piece of the ball, the second baseman another, and the shortstop the third.

For a split second there was confusion. The runner on second, going with the crack of the bat, had scored easily. The batter stood perched on first. But Niles had caught the ball, even though it took three players to do it.

The umpire never hesitated. With the wind beginning to howl and rain coming faster and harder, he raced to the mound. Above the roar of the storm I could just barely make out his words.

"Three players caught a piece of the ball," he yelled above the rising crescendo of the storm. "But when the lightning struck the ball I saw fragments of it hit the ground. The rule states that if any part of the ball hits the ground it is considered a hit. Since the entire ball was not caught, the runner is safe at first, the run scores, and Edwardsburg wins the game, two to one."

The storm, perhaps waiting for the decision itself, exploded in all its fury then. The skies opened in a deluge of rain that, driven by gale-force winds, had everyone drenched in seconds.

We all raced for our cars then, but it was impossible to drive anywhere in that kind of weather. Surely a tornado had been near, as awesome as the storm was.

I had plenty of time to think, sitting there in my car. And it suddenly hit me — like a bolt of lightning, so to speak — that I had witnessed the greatest decision ever made by an umpire.

● ● ●

Gadget plays can be nasty on umpires. Some trickery is involved in most, and if an umpire doesn't have his mind completely in the game, he could miss something. Trick plays are designed to fool the opposition. But as I have said, I was never the angel of the ball diamond, and I didn't hesitate to capitalize on the umpires when I could. One of my favorite umpire stories happened when I was playing with the Fostoria Redbirds. It gave a whole new meaning to the ole "hidden ball" play.

I told George Silvey, the manager of the Redbirds, that I had a great play that would win us a ballgame someday. George thought it was bush, but I said, "What the hell? If it wins us a game, who cares if it's bush or not?"

George never did like the idea, but he didn't stop me either. All he said was that if the play didn't work it would cost me five dollars, big money in those days.

My idea was a spinoff of the "hidden ball" play. I knew it would take a long time to set it up, and would work only once, but I went ahead with it anyway.

My plan revolved around "Red" Jenkins, a redheaded pitcher

we had on the team. Red would believe anything he heard and do anything you asked. He fit my plan perfectly because he was left-handed, and because he was the only guy to fall for my scheme.

Red and I began working on the play about midseason. Every time Red was on the mound and there was a man on second, I'd call time, stroll to the mound and chat for a while, and sneak the ball into my glove. As I passed the umpire on the way back to my position, I'd whisper to him that I had the ball. It was usually pretty obvious that I'd taken the ball from Red, so the umpire would just nod and the runner would be hugging second. I'd throw the ball back to Red and we'd keep playing.

For five or six weeks Red and I kept acting out our little drama, sometimes three and four times a game. And after a while the umpires (our Class D league used just two umpires a game and we often had the same crews over and over) became used to our little routine.

Everything to that point, though, had been for show, a con to set up the real thing. Finally, it came.

Late in the season we were leading a team 8-7. They had one out and a runner on second. I called time and told George to bring in Jenkins. We could use a lefthander in that situation, but really I wanted to pull my plan and Red would know what to do.

After Red completed his warmups I sauntered to the mound, as I had done so many times before, and snuck the ball into my glove. This time, though, I slipped the ball back to Red. Then I headed for my position, telling the ump I had the ball as I passed him.

Red stood on the mound checking his signals, his arms at his sides. The runner on second could clearly see the ball in his glove but the umpire, positioned just to the other side of the mound, couldn't. Red went into his stretch and held it, the runner took his lead, and suddenly I lunged at him and slapped him with my glove.

"Yer out!" the ump yelled.

The runner screamed bloody murder, but before he could get the umpire to check my glove I raced to the mound and pretended to give the ball back to Red. "Accidentally" we let it fall to the ground between us, and there was nothing they could do.

I never tried the play again. Word got around and besides, I knew it would only work once. For some odd reason, the umpires in that league never really trusted me after that.

● ● ●

I pulled a similar trick in my earlier days, though it wasn't as dramatic. We were playing in Eau Claire, Wisconsin, and I was with the Grand Forks, Minnesota, team playing in the Northern League. Our games usually didn't start until almost six and many times weren't over until well after dark. This was just small-time ball and the diamonds didn't have lights, so it got kind of dangerous at times.

We were ahead by a run going into the seventh inning and already it was getting dark. I was notorious for getting on umpires anyway and had been ragging the crew all night about cutting the game short. But the more I bitched the more they bristled. The game was supposed to be nine innings and, damnit, that's what we were going to play.

Neither team scored in the seventh, and the eighth opened darker still. The outfielders were blurs and it was hard to see the ball clearly until it was a few feet from you. Either reason took over then, or else the umpires just wanted to shut me up, but they announced that the eighth inning would be the last.

We didn't score in our half of the inning; hell, you could hardly see the ball. But the other team chopped a few that we lost in the gloom and loaded the bases with two outs. Their next hitter was their stud, the team's big home run man. Our pitcher got two strikes on him, and I could see the kid was having trouble picking up the ball, but he still scared me. All he had to do was meet the ball and we'd lose it for sure in the dark.

So I called time out and waved the catcher out to the mound. I told the pitcher to give the catcher the ball and not to worry. All he had to do was go through his motion and make his delivery. Then I told the catcher to hide the ball and, when the pitcher made his delivery, pop it into his glove. Then we all returned to our positions.

It came off without a hitch. A split second after the pitcher made his delivery, I heard a loud thud from behind the plate, then the umpire's voice loud and clear, "Strike three."

Both teams happened to be staying at the same hotel and later I asked the kid how he could stand there with the bases loaded and take a pitch right down the middle.

"Don't kid me, Lucadello," he said. "I got cheated. You know as well as I do that that pitch was at least a foot outside."

• • •

Major league ballplayers and umpires have their own secret interaction that rarely if ever leaves the playing field. In the many years I've followed the major leagues, however, I've found out about some of the little tête-à-têtes that occur on the diamond.

There was the time, one umpire told me, when the score was 2-1, the tying run was on second, and there was one away. The batter looped a Texas leaguer into short centerfield and the runner, thinking it would drop in, took off. The centerfielder made a great shoestring catch, though, then fired to second to double off the runner by a good ten feet.

The umpire, who had run out into centerfield to make sure whether the ball was caught or not, signaled the batter out but the runner safe.

The centerfielder exploded, charging the umpire and erupting into a real eyeball-to-eyeball rhubarb.

"How could you make a call like that?" he screamed. "You had your back to the play."

The umpire, unabashed, just smiled.

"John," he said. "For ten years now you've been telling me I got my eyes in my ass. If you still believe that, then I had a great view of the play."

• • •

Umpires don't always agree among themselves, but they invariably work out a solution.

I heard of the time, for instance, when the major league umpires were asked to attend spring training with the players. Then, like the players, they could get some game situation practice in before the season.

But the umpires were split on the issue. The younger ones liked the idea because in between ballgames they could get in some golf, check out the beaches, and generally forget about the cold up north.

The older umpires, though, more set and stubborn in their ways, didn't savor the idea of putting in that much work before the season even started. One of their group, who carried a lot of weight in the organization, was especially adamant about not going.

The stalemate was at an impasse when one little exchange broke the tension.

"George," one of the younger men said, "why don't you want

to go to spring training? What's the real reason?"

"Well, I'll tell you," said the older gentleman. "They say most of those parks down in Florida are near lakes and marshes that are full of snakes. They say sometimes the fields are just covered with them. What happens if I get bit by a water moccasin or some other poisonous snake?"

"Don't worry, George. All the umpires will have little medicine kits with razor blades and bandages and stuff. If you get bit, we'll just cut it open, suck out the poison, and bandage you right up."

"Sure," the older one said. "And what if I get bit in the ass?"

"In that case," the young man shot back, "you find out real damn quick who your best friends are."

The Wall

Matt Stone is a definite prospect, no doubt about it. The Wayne, Ohio, standout has it all — a strong and accurate arm, excellent fielding fundamentals, and the sweetest swing around.

It came as no surprise last year that when an all-star tournament came up, Matt was elevated to a higher division and still excelled. The kid's a talent. He's dedicated. He's sound. He's a quality ballplayer.

Matt Stone is also nine years old.

Two years ago Matt Stone wouldn't have been allowed to carry the bats onto the same fields he would later star on with a team of players two and three years older than he. Matt Stone, though, is living testimony to a concept very dear to Tony Lucadello. Lucadello called it "The Wall," and in its simple design may lie the answer to one of baseball's most complicated questions.

The quality of the ballplayers entering the colleges and big leagues has diminished tremendously in the past fifteen to twenty years. The standards of baseball have gone backwards.

Coaches are having to teach nineteen- and twenty-year-olds fundamental basics they should have mastered long before. Such an emphasis has been put on winning, especially at the lower levels, that the word "practice" has been virtually eliminated from the vocabulary. The word "practice" is what's missing from our entire amateur system.

If you're going to build talent you have to start early, with boys five, six, seven years old. You can't start at the top and work down. You have to start at the bottom and work up. You have to lay that strong foundation, and in my opinion, "The Wall" is where we have to start.

The Wall is a simple thing, really. Six feet high and six feet wide is all it need be. For a truer bounce it should be made of concrete blocks and should have a short slope and the base for popups. Add a ball and a small boy with a little interest, and you're in business.

Think of the possibilities. One boy can practice alone, and it's right in the boy's own backyard. Say he throws that ball against that wall 100 times a day, or 200 times, or 300. Every time he throws he's improving his arm and his accuracy. And, of course, he has to field each throw so he learns the basics of staying down on the ball, fielding it cleanly, and getting set for another throw.

That's what I mean by practice. Say that same boy belonged to a Little League or Pony League team. Even if there were only eleven or twelve boys on the team, there's no possible way each one could be given 100 ground balls or make 100 throws to a certain spot.

Kids used to be able to bounce a ball off the side of a barn or the side of the house. And there always seemed to be an empty lot where they could get up a game. But they build apartment houses or office buildings on the vacant lots now. Not too many kids live on farms anymore, and I don't think their parents would like them throwing a ball against the aluminum siding on the house.

The Wall is the perfect solution.

When I covered four states, Ohio, Indiana, Michigan, and Kentucky, I noticed, especially in Indiana and Kentucky, that almost every house had a basketball rim, either on a pole in the driveway or nailed onto a garage or barn. I didn't think it was just coincidence that Indiana and Kentucky turn out some of the best basketball players in the country. I took the same basic philosophy and applied it to another sport.

Someone — a mother, a father, a friend, or neighbor — can stand off to the side and loft whiffle balls for the boy to hit. Whiffle balls won't fly that far anyway, but if he hits them off the wall they'd be right there. Then he could pick them up and hit them again.

The whole idea is very inexpensive. The wall itself wouldn't cost that much, and whiffle balls are cheap.

The potential for a young ballplayer, though, is priceless. Imagine a young boy throwing and fielding a couple hundred balls a day and getting in 100 swings of the bat. It would be impossible for him to get that same amount of experience in a regular team practice.

Say a boy started when he was five and did that for five years. By the time he was ten he would have the fundamentals down pat. You wouldn't have to teach him how to throw or field or hit. You could concentrate on the details of the game of baseball, not the fundamentals.

If all young ballplayers, say between the ages of five and ten, started following this program now, the decline in the quality of ballplayers could be solved in five years. Something has to be done, and the time to start is now.

In Wayne, Ohio, there is living proof of Lucadello's plan.

"When he was eight he was just your average eight-year-old ballplayer," Matt's mother Judy said. *"But he and a neighborhood friend, Casey Shultz, practiced a full year on that wall. If it wasn't raining too hard or too much snow on the ground, they were out there.*

"We were surprised he hit nine home runs this season, but when they promoted him from Class C ball to B and he played well even against the older boys, well, then I knew it was worth it."

"I was excited about getting The Wall," Matt said. *"I didn't think it was work or nothing. It was fun. Casey would come over and we'd pretend we'd have real games and everything."*

"I was amazed at the improvement in Matt's control and throwing," Gene Stone said of his son. *"Even after the first few weeks I could see he was throwing harder and with greater accuracy."*

The Wall had, for Gene Stone, other benefits.

"It only cost around fifty dollars and I completed it in a few nights after work," he said. *"But what I really like is that it's right here in our backyard. We don't have to worry about what could happen if he was alone on the schoolyard or somewhere."*

Matt Stone's isn't the only documented case for Lucadello's wall. In

1981, Dave Kitchell, sports editor of the Kokomo Tribune, *did an article on what he called "brickball." And to test the effectiveness of the theory he tried it on his seven-year-old son Ryan.*

At a local schoolyard, father and son put the plan into action. Kitchell noted that his son cleanly fielded 59 of 100 chances the first day, but improved his performance to 90 of 100 by the end of the week.

Kitchell made some important observations from the experience, such as the need for The Wall to be close at hand and readily available; the need for parents to keep from pressing the child and making use of The Wall an obligation; flexibility in equipment (a whiffle ball for beginners, tennis ball for intermediates, and later a regulation baseball); the need for a continuous challenge so the child steadily can improve; and above all, that it should be fun.

"I have seven guys who work for me," Lucadello once told Kitchell. "As a group we see 30,000 players a year. This year [1981] we saw four who had major league potential . . . only four."

It's a problem that Lucadello's Wall can help correct. So far, though, it's been a rather quiet campaign.

"If they would plug it on national TV during the baseball season or get two major leaguers to push it or get the endorsement of the commissioner, it would probably catch on like wildfire," Lucadello said.

"What burns me is to hear a young boy say 'Come on, Dad, let's throw,' and the dad says, 'Can't son, haven't got the time.' I realize many parents can't spare the time, but here's a plan, an opportunity for them to do something. It's simple, inexpensive, and it works. Matt Stone is living proof of that."

Afterword

It was the spring of 1971, and on a small-town baseball diamond a seventeen-year-old shortstop was fielding grounders. He wouldn't have noticed the man by the thirdbase dugout, except for the Sunday-go-to-meeting way he was dressed: coat and tie, overcoat, and his trademark, a houndstooth hat. It wasn't long until after practice that Coach told the team who he was: Tony Lucadello, baseball scout for the Philadelphia Phillies.

Major league scouts are big news at a Class A school. Lucadello had probably seen every ball diamond from Ada to Zanesville, but it didn't matter. He'd been at that field on that day, and every player on the team probably wondered if he was the one Lucadello would remember.

What, the shortstop wondered, would a report on him say? Good glove. Average bat. Speed? Runs like a furniture mover with a baby grand on his back. Oh well. He'd been "seen" by a major league scout. And seventeen-year-old shortstops thrive on big league dreams.

It was the spring of 1979, and a twenty-five-year-old sportswriter was covering the Class A regional semifinals at Patrick Henry High School. Rain had already postponed the tournament twice, and an overcast sky was threatening to do so again.

Behind the backstop, though, laughter bubbled.

A small, well-dressed man was holding court for coaches and fans alike, and as the sportswriter approached he heard unfold a remarkable tale of a minor league ballplayer who once played for the Fostoria Redbirds.

The player, so the story went, was in center field one game when the opposition's clean-up hitter belted one deep. The center fielder raced back, stood on the fence, and reached over. He couldn't get to the ball, but at the last moment a pigeon flew into the path of the ball, got nailed, and fell into the player's glove.

Thinking fast, the player closed the glove and turned it toward the umpire, who saw a bit of white through the leather and called the batter out. Later, when the rest of the team learned the truth, they returned to the field, dug up home plate, and buried the bird beneath it.

That minor league player was Tony Lucadello, the same man telling the story. The sportswriter didn't remember the name, but there was something familiar about the man's houndstooth hat.

The spring sports season ended, and there were no more high school events for the sportswriter to cover. So one day, looking for something with a local angle, he wrote a story about that famous catch, telling the tale in much the same way Lucadello himself had.

A short time later he received a call.

"This is Tony Lucadello," the man said, "For years people have asked me to do a book on my experiences as a baseball scout. I liked the way you wrote that story about the catch, and I want you to do the book."

And so began a business relationship that grew into friendship.

Awed at first, the sportswriter was more than a little impressed by Lucadello's track record. In over forty-five years as a scout for the Chicago Cubs and Philadelphia Phillies, Lucadello had signed more major league players than any other scout — forty-nine by last count.

Some of the game's great players signed their first contract with Lucadello, including Mike Schmidt, Fergie Jenkins, Alex Johnson, Mike Marshall, Larry Hisle, Toby Harrah, Grant Jackson, Terry Harmon, Tom Underwood, Dave Roberts, Barry Bonnell, Jim Essian, Larry Cox, Eddie Haas, Dick Drott, Don Elston, and Jim Brosnan. Their faces and more dotted the walls of Lucadello's West Center Street basement office. He'd point at one, lean back in his chair, and say, "Take Mike Marshall there. Let me tell you about how I signed him . . ."

There would be stories — weird, wild, wonderful tales from the past. The tape recorder would whirr, the sportswriter would listen, and music would fill the room.

It is the spring of 1989. And it is a cold, empty spring. Tony

Lucadello went to the ballpark Monday. And there lies the irony, for on the field that gave him his zest for life, he took his own.

Never a man to seek personal recognition, Lucadello earned it nonetheless when he put a .32-caliber pistol to his mouth and pulled the trigger.

It ended his life, but not his legacy. Not for the men he signed to play baseball, not for the high school and college players who will someday replace them, and not for the youngsters who are just now learning about the game he loved. And not for a sportswriter who once wrote all the right words. The words don't come easy now.

— DAVID V. HANNEMAN

Some of Tony's

"boys"

FRED ANDREWS

DICK DROTT

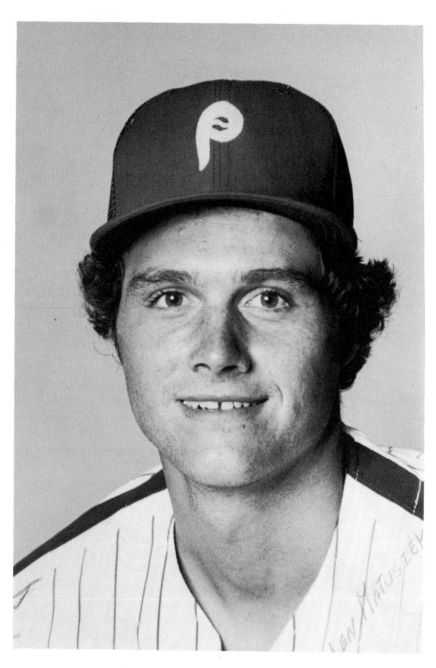

LEN MATUSZEK

MIKE MARSHALL

JOHN UPHAM

JOHNNY LUCADELLO

SCOTT MUNNINGHOFF

JIM ESSIAN

BARRY BONNELL

DAVE ROBERTS

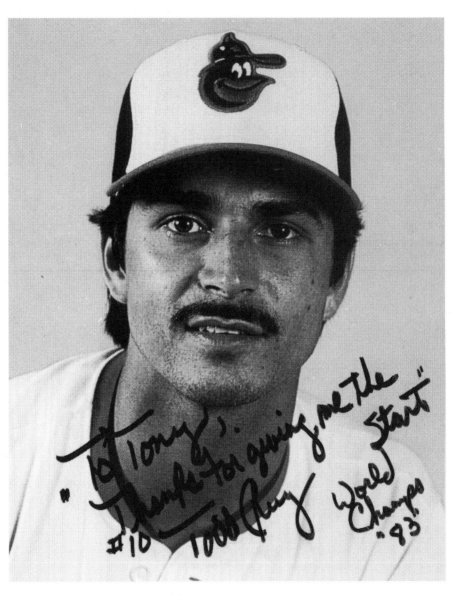

TODD CRUZ

GRANT JACKSON

TOBY HARRAH

ALEX JOHNSON

TOM UNDERWOOD

FERGIE JENKINS

To Philadelphia's
greatest scout and
to the great man
who has helped me
become the ball player
I am today— Tony
Lucadello

from
Larry Hisle

LARRY HISLE

TERRY HARMON

LARRY COX

MIKE SCHMIDT

34
34
34
―――
112
54
―――
26 6

$66
26+
100
65
$1
―――
59 7